THE WESTWARD MOVEMENT IN THE UNITED STATES

RAY ALLEN BILLINGTON

William Smith Mason Professor of History
Northwestern University

AN ANVIL ORIGINAL

under the general editorship of

LOUIS L. SNYDER

D. VAN NOSTRAND COMPANY, INC.

PRINCETON, NEW JERSEY

TORONTO   LONDON

NEW YORK

For Anne and André Bader

973
B496wて
cop. 24
His

D. VAN NOSTRAND COMPANY, INC.
120 Alexander St., Princeton, New Jersey (*Principal office*); 24 West 40 St., New York, N.Y.
D. VAN NOSTRAND COMPANY (Canada), LTD.
25 Hollinger Rd., Toronto 16, Canada
D. VAN NOSTRAND COMPANY, LTD.
358, Kensington High Street, London, W.14, England

Library of Congress Catalog Card No. 59-9757

PRINTED IN THE UNITED STATES OF AMERICA

PREFACE

THE compression of the mountainous quantities of information relating to the American frontier into a book of this size may be accomplished either by describing in detail a number of selected events which can merge in the reader's mind to create an impression of the whole, something as the dots in a half-tone blend to form a composite image, or by writing in general terms with little attention to specific episodes. The former technique is misleading unless the events selected are exactly typical; the latter sacrifices the color and glamor inherent in human behavior by its emphasis on sweeping statements or generalizations. Rather than risk creating an inaccurate impression, I have chosen the latter method for this book, hoping that those who read it will not be misled by my oversimplification of a complex migration pattern but will be encouraged to explore its actual complexities in the longer volumes listed at the close of the documentary section.

My purpose has been to follow the moving frontier westward across the United States from the beginning of Anglo-American settlement to the 1890's when the pioneering era was drawing to a close. The resulting pattern is both chronological and geographical, with emphasis on the latter. Thus I have pictured the occupation of the Mississippi Valley before dealing with the movement of frontiersmen into the trans-Mississippi West, even though the two occurred simultaneously. It is to be hoped that this method, faulty though it may be, will reveal something of the tribulations of the pioneers as they moved doggedly toward the Pacific, and that it will emphasize the ingenuity with which they adapted to the mosaic of differing environments that they conquered. For this, in essence, explains the America that the frontier helped create.

Evanston, Illinois　　　　　RAY ALLEN BILLINGTON
February, 1959

TABLE OF CONTENTS

Part I

THE WESTWARD MOVEMENT IN THE UNITED STATES

— 1 —

INTRODUCTION

No single force has been responsible for the unique pattern of American history or for the distinguishing characteristics of the American people, but of the many that have contributed—the mingling of races from many lands, the diversified economy, the belated but highly accelerated industrialization of the nation—none played a more essential role than the westward movement of the frontier. For the three centuries needed to settle the continent, pioneers marched toward the setting sun in a never-ending procession. As they moved they not only sent a flow of newly tapped natural resources eastward to revitalize the economy, but developed new artifacts, institutions, and habits suited to life in thinly settled communities. Many of these have persisted since the passing of the frontier to endow the United States with the most distinctive features of its civilization.

The Settlement Pattern. This westward march followed a set pattern. On the cutting edge of the moving frontier roamed fur traders and trappers, to spy out the riches of the West and report their discoveries to those who waited behind. Next, when conditions were ripe, came the miners, to pan streams from Georgia to California in their ceaseless search for the tell-tale glint of gold, and to build their rough mining camps wherever a "strike" was made. Not far behind were the cattlemen, constantly seeking grasslands where their herds could roam freely without the hindrance of farmers' fences.

Ranchers fattened beeves in the "cowpens" of seventeenth-century Virginia and Massachusetts, or on the lush prairies of Illinois, long before the cowboy became king of the open range in the Far West. None of these three frontier types made a permanent impression on the wilderness; they were bent on skimming off surface wealth rather than rearing enduring settlements.

Those who followed over the trails they blazed had a different purpose. Some were speculators, roaming far in advance of the frontier to usurp town sites or rich farm lands that would command a high price when pioneers moved in. More were "pioneer farmers" seeking the wealth that fate or indolence had denied them at home; these nomads usually "squatted" on the land rather than buying, built a crude cabin, started a small clearing, and then sold their "improvements" to move on again as neighbors pressed in upon them. Their purchasers were "equipped farmers" who intended to remain; they cleared away the forest, grubbed out stumps, built frame houses, fenced their fields, and labored on the roads that would end their isolation. Over these highways came other pioneer types to settle nearby: grist-millers, distillers, merchants, lawyers, country editors, and a host of others alert to the profits awaiting those who could provide needed services for the expanding community. Their coming signaled the end of the pioneering period, for as their villages merged with the "East" that lay behind, the frontier passed on to begin the conquest of a newer "West."

Reasons for Migration.   Whether land-hungry farmers or cash-hungry lawyers, the pioneers shared one thing in common: all were drawn westward by the magnet of opportunity or the lure of adventure. Some moved when their lands were worn thin by successive plantings or when prices in the East precluded buying the extra acres needed to support an ever-growing family. Others left when neighbors pressed too closely upon them; an eighteenth-century farmer in Connecticut reported that his friends were leaving for the West "that they may have more Room, thinking that we live too thick." Still others responded to the call of the unknown, or migrated (as one group did in early Massachusetts) because they "felt a strong bent of their spirits for change." But self-improvement economically and socially was the incentive that lured most men westward, and the hope of self-improvement has bulked large in the American dream from that day to this.

Those who felt this urge were largely farmers who lived not far from the frontier, for distance, the expenses of pioneering, and a lack of essential skills kept most eastern laborers or city dwellers at home. New Englanders moved into western New York, their sons pressed on into Michigan and Illinois, their grandsons into Iowa and Nebraska. "In thirty states out of thirty-four," wrote the Superintendent of the Census in 1860, ". . . the native emigrants have chiefly preferred to locate in a State immediately adjacent to that of their birth." Younger sons of nearby farmers, anxious for a home of their own and unable to afford the higher-priced lands in well-settled communities, fed the frontier stream as did no other group.

These were the pioneers who cleared away the forests and subdued the grasslands of the American West. Some found illusive fortune in their new homes and stayed to prosper; others failed and drifted westward time and time again before succumbing to hardship and poverty. But all contributed to the epic of conquest by which a continent was won and a nation endowed with a faith in progress that has remained an essential ingredient of its strength.

— 2 —

THE COLONIAL FRONTIER, 1607–1763

When Anglo-American frontiersmen in the early seventeenth century began their conquest of the wilderness that was to become the United States, other Europeans had already staked their claims to a large portion of the continent. Their presence not only stimulated England's interest in the New World, but helped shape the course of settlement for a century to come.

The Spanish Borderlands. The Spaniards, with a prior claim stemming from Columbus' discovery, were first on the scene. Naturally assuming that the mystery-shrouded wilds of North America concealed wealth comparable to that found among the Aztecs of Mexico and the Incas of Peru (1519-1528), they launched a series of exploring expeditions during the early sixteenth century, all of which ended in disaster. Álvar Ñuñez Cabeza de Vaca marched along the Gulf of Mexico from the Floridas to the west coast of Mexico between 1528 and 1536, with nothing but tales of incredible hardship to show for his efforts. Undiscouraged by de Vaca's straightforward account of the barren country that he had traversed, Hernando de Soto, a wealthy nobleman, in 1539 began the wanderings that ended in his burial in the mighty river that he had discovered, the Mississippi, four years later. Far to the West Francisco Vásquez de Coronado added a tale of unbelievable adventure to the annals of exploration by leading his followers from Mexico City to modern Kansas before returning, a broken man (1540-1542). The findings of these three tragic expeditions were all the same: North America concealed neither the precious metals nor the native souls that interested Spain in the New World.

Yet the North American continent could not be neglected, as the French dramatically proved in 1565 when they founded an outpost on the east Florida coast to raid Spanish treasure galleons as they sailed by on the homeward route. Clearly, Spaniards reasoned, the borderlands surrounding the riches of Mexico and Central America must be occupied. Soldiers proved inadequate to the task, but the formula that proved successful was discovered in 1593 when a handful of Franciscan missionaries landed in Florida. Within a dozen years the Indian converts grouped about their mission stations numbered in the thousands, all of them busily learning the arts of civilization as well as Christianity as they were transformed into Spanish citizens by the devout friars. Other missionaries were sent northward from Mexico to begin their labors in New Mexico (1598), Arizona (1700), and Texas (1716). As their stations multiplied, and as farmers and ranchers drifted in to exploit the countryside, these buffer areas became firmly attached to the orbit of Spain's empire. Her hold on the northern provinces was by no means secure, but for the time being the southern boundary of the area open to Anglo-American pioneers had been delineated.

The Frontier of New France. Far to the north other Europeans were marking the northern limits of the domain that Englishmen were free to occupy. French interest in the New World began when her fishermen, long accustomed to visiting the Newfoundland banks for cod and halibut, discovered that natives along the Canadian shore would trade great bales of beaver pelts for a few beads or a broken mirror. Thus was born the fur trade, on which France built her American empire. For a time the trade was haphazard, but in 1603 it became a crown monopoly; at the same time the man destined to shape the course of French expansion, Samuel de Champlain, entered the picture. First from a tiny outpost on St. Croix island, and after 1608 from the village of Quebec that he founded beneath the St. Lawrence's towering cliffs, Champlain directed the activities that were to win his monarch both Canada and the entire interior of the continent.

The fur trade was the tool used by this canny empire-builder. Knowing that profits mounted amazingly as relations were established with unsophisticated interior tribes unfamiliar with the value of the white man's pots and blankets and guns and brandy, and aware that every new trading alliance meant French control of a new segment of the interior, Champlain sent his "Young Men" constantly westward in their quest for furs. By the end of the 1630's they had pioneered the Ottawa River-Lake Nipissing water route to the upper Great Lakes, discovered the Straits of Mackinac, and were found among the red men of Wisconsin's Green Bay country. A few years later they had extended the frontiers of New France into the lands bordering Lake Superior. Wherever they went, they won the country with the Indians; France controlled Canada as firmly as did the Spaniards the borderland fringing the Gulf of Mexico. Between these two embryo empires was a wilderness containing neither surface gold nor prime pelts. In this less-attractive land, Anglo-American pioneers planted the seeds of an empire that would eventually engulf the entire continent.

Englishmen on the Tidewater Frontier. The British pioneers who founded their first outpost at Jamestown in Virginia in 1607 were to learn by bitter experience that the customs of their homeland, where men were many and land scarce, were ill-suited to the New World where the opposite situation prevailed. So they endured a "Starving time" as workers refused to labor on company farms as company servants, producing items because they were wanted in the mother country rather than because they would command a profit. As these lessons were learned, land was divided among the settlers to till as they chose, a "head right" system introduced to encourage migration by granting fifty-acre plots to all paying the passage of a newcomer, and the culture of highly profitable tobacco encouraged. Thus did Englishmen respond to the frontier environment by recognizing that individual enterprise provided the best inducement for workers in areas where natural resources were abundant, and that land grants were the surest magnets to attract settlers. Maryland, a second colony founded in 1632, followed Virginia's example so successfully that its pioneers endured no "Starving time."

With these lessons learned, expansion followed rapidly, first westward along the valleys of the James, Chickahominy, Rappahannock, and Potomac rivers as far as the "fall line" where rapids stopped navigation, then over the highlands that separated these streams. By the 1660's the southern coastal plain, or Tidewater, was filling with small farms growing corn and tobacco. Within this area, small though it was, a number of distinct zones were discernible, each representing a transitional stage in the emergence of civilization. Along the "fall line" lived a handful of "border barons" whose log forts served as headquarters for fur traders who were yearly pressing farther into the unknown interior. Near them herdsmen pastured their cattle, drifting from peavine march to peavine march as the grass wore thin or farmers approached. Still farther east was a land of small farmers, busily engaged in girdling the trees, planting maize among the still-standing stumps, and slowly pushing back the wilderness. Heavily in debt and burdened with the poverty normal in a new country, they were distrustful of the larger farmers whose "plantations" characterized the more mature society near the coast. Although the large plantation was yet unknown to the South, the relatively greater wealth of the seaboard planters encouraged a social snobbery that made them, in turn, view the interior farmers with open disdain.

These antagonisms bore fruit in Bacon's Rebellion, the first of the many conflicts between East and West that marked the frontier's westward movement. Trouble began along the Virginia fall line where the small farmers, their poverty deepened by declining tobacco prices during the 1660's and their pride offended by the demands of aristocratic Easterners that all voice in the government be denied them, were goaded into revolt when the governor refused to sanction their plans to seize Indian lands by force. In this mood they took matters into their own hands during the spring of 1676. Choosing a young Whig, Nathaniel Bacon, as their leader, they sent an unauthorized army to attack the Indians, then marched on Jamestown to seize control of the colony by force. Bacon died when his rebellion was at its height, allowing the authorities to punish the rebels with such viciousness that even the English monarch recoiled, but the spirit of resistance did not die with him. Many of his followers fled southward, to begin new homes in the colony of Carolina that had just been founded there.

The Early New England Frontier. While some Englishmen transformed the southern Tidewater into a land of yellow tobacco fields, others pushed back the forests of New England to create a new and markedly different social order. From Plymouth and Boston, settled in Massachusetts Bay Colony in 1620 and 1630 by religious dissenters from England's established Anglican Church, these pioneers moved into the interior much in the manner of their counterparts in the South. The coastal lowlands were occupied first, then the valley of the Connecticut River where such towns as Hartford, Wethersfield, Windsor, and Springfield were founded in the mid-1630's. Others drifted southward to build their homes near Rhode Island's Narragansett Bay at Providence or Warwick or Newport, or moved northward along the Merrimac River into New Hampshire. They, too, found that Indian resistance mounted as they advanced, forcing them to fight the Pequot War (1637) which virtually exterminated that tribe.

Yet the differences between the northern and southern frontiers were more notable than the similarities. Southerners moved as individuals, sought the best land with no concern for its proximity to other settlements, purchased from speculators or with "head rights," cleared their own fields, and turned as rapidly as possible to tobacco production for foreign markets. New Englanders migrated in groups, selected town sites adjacent to existing communities, secured their lands free from the legislatures, worked together to subdue the forest, and concentrated on the growth of cereals and livestock for local consumption. For these differences in pioneering techniques both geographic conditions and differing religious beliefs were responsible.

To the devout Puritans who reared their wilderness Zion in New England, profits were less important than the perpetuation of God's true faith. Hence, they agreed that the "sitting down of men" should be entrusted to the legislatures, with the understanding that free grants be made to all orthodox believers willing to settle in groups near their ministers and churches. Whenever such a group applied for land, its members were made the "proprietors" of a town site about six miles square; in return for this grant they were expected to survey the plot into fields, lay out a village "green," build a church and school, and grant homesites to newcomers without charge. The fields were then cleared by community effort, a "common" for pasturage fenced, and cultivation begun, with each Puritan tilling his land by day and returning to his home in the village by night. As town site after town site was granted and improved, orderly tiers of settlement pushed back the wilderness, assuring the New Englanders less loneliness and greater protection from Indians than any other frontiersmen in history.

Strong as were the religious ties responsible for New England's unique land system, they could not have endured had natural conditions been more favorable. Frontiersmen able to profit by exploiting nature's riches could never be kept in check, as the South's helter-skelter settlement pattern demonstrated, but in the Puritan colonies a hilly countryside, thin soils, and rock-strewn fields doomed them to backbreaking toil with scant returns. Unable to grow the prized staples of agriculture—tobacco, sugar, cotton, rice, or indigo—they felt no compulsion to seek fertile lands or amass large holdings. Instead they were content to obey the dictates of their church, and to be satisfied with self-sufficiency and salvation in lieu of wealth.

Seventeenth-Century Expansion of New England. The land system did encourage a steady if unspectacular migration westward by assuring frontiersmen protection from the Indians, sure land titles, and less hardship than was the usual lot of the pioneer. It also served as an expelling force by fomenting trouble between the town proprietors and later-comers who were known as "freemen" or "cottagers." As the latter group increased in each community until its members were in a majority, a demand for a further division of the town lands inevitably followed. This the proprietors resisted, seeking instead to retain control against the day when profits could be secured by sale. These disputes normally ended in the courts with the proprietors triumphant and the disgruntled losers moving on to newer towns where a thickening population had not yet fostered a speculative spirit among the owners.

This westward-shifting population over-ran the lowlands of New England between 1640 and 1675. In Maine and New Hampshire settlements still clung to the coastal plain, but in Massachusetts river bottoms filled rapidly, especially that of the Connecticut as far north as Deerfield and Northfield. In Rhode Island towns extended along the Blackstone Valley to Woonsocket and Seekonk, while Connecticut's settled areas embraced the New Haven backcountry and reached northwestward from New London into lands bordering the Thames River.

This pattern spelled trouble, for caught between the advancing columns of pioneers were a number of Indian tribes: the Narragansetts and Wampanoags of Rhode Island, and the Mohegans and Podunks of the Connecticut Valley. Knowing that they must strike back to protect their shrinking hunting grounds, the red men rallied under King Philip, a Wampanoag chief, and in the spring of 1675 fell upon the settlers. For two years King Philip's War raged with such fury that even such easterly towns as Providence and Boston looked to their defenses; when it ended in 1677 New England had lost one-sixth of its male population and twenty-five towns had been destroyed. Yet the result was inevitable. The defeat of King Philip and his followers re-opened the gates for a new westward push of the frontier.

The Advance Into the "Old West." By this time pioneers were ready to begin their assault on the physiographic province known as the "Old West." Lying west of the "fall line," and comprising the rugged foothills and fertile interior valleys of the 1,300-mile long Applachian Mountain Range, this section provided a setting for frontier expansion unlike any faced by earlier settlers. In its forest-choked valleys, cut off from direct communication with Europe or even the East, they were to live under conditions more primitive than their ancestors had known and to respond by developing traits and institutions that marked them as typically American.

The first portion of the Old West to be occupied was

the Southern Piedmont, a land of hills and valleys sloping upward to join the towering Blue Ridge at the eastern border of the mountains. During the 1670's and
1680's exploring expeditions sent out by Captain Abraham Wood and other fur traders who commanded the
forts along Virginia's "fall line" brought back tales of
rich valley lands lying deep in the interior (*see Document
No. 1*), and, as the word spread, farmers left disgruntled
by the collapse of Bacon's Rebellion began following
their trails westward. The movement was hurried in the
waning years of the seventeenth century by the spread of
plantations in the older sections of Virginia and Maryland, with the resulting displacement of small land hold-
ers. By 1710 this migration was in full tide, and with it a
rush to the Piedmont of wealthy planter-speculators
anxious to engross the best fields against the day when
they could be resold at a profit. So rapid was the influx
that settlements extended as far west as the Blue Ridge
by 1740, and were ready to push beyond into the Shenandoah Valley.

When they did so the westward-moving Virginians and
Carolinians met another population stream moving southward from New York and Pennsylvania. These colonies
had been only recently occupied by England, New York
by the conquest of its Dutch owners in 1664, Pennsylvania through the efforts of its Quaker founder, William
Penn, in 1681. Conditions in the former colony discouraged expansion, for the fur traders, who carried on a
thriving traffic with the Iroquois Indians of the Mohawk
Valley from their headquarters at Albany, were influential enough to keep settlers out of the backcountry, but
in Pennsylvania the situation was just the opposite. The
liberal proprietor opened the doors of his colony to the
oppressed of all the world, attracting such an army of
newcomers that they soon spilled over into the beckoning
lands that lay to the south. Their coming added both
strength and color to the entire backcountry.

**The Occupation of the Great Valley of the Appa-
lachians.** In the van were peasants from the Rhinish
Palatinate of Germany, driven from their tiny farms by
devastating wars and plundering princelings. Hearing that
England was seeking settlers for its colonies, a little band

of Palatines reached London in 1708 and realized their dreams when the government sent them to New York to produce naval stores. Their success sets the tide running; by 1709 some 13,500 of them were waiting in England to be shipped overseas and each year thereafter the number increased as those in America wrote enthusiastically of a land "where the farmers or husbandmen live better than lords." Lack of opportunity in New York soon deflected the stream to Pennsylvania where Germans filled the broad Susquehanna Valley with their tidy homes and their substantial "Palatine Barns," and where their ancestors remain today as the "Pennsylvania Dutch." As the valley filled, the stream turned southward along the natural highway that led them into Virginia's Shenandoah Valley, then southward still into the North Carolina backcountry. By mid-eighteenth century a band of German settlements stretched along the Great Valley of the Appalachians from the Schoharie country of northern New York to the borders of South Carolina.

There they were joined by a second stream of migrants from abroad, the Scots-Irish whose source was Ulster in northern Ireland. Composed of the descendants of Scottish Presbyterians who had pioneered that country a century before, Englishmen and Irishmen, these sturdy peasants had been displaced by British laws that disrupted their economy and interfered with their religious practices. As they began their mass movement toward America about 1717, Pennsylvania proved to be the mecca that attracted most; like the Germans they concentrated in the interior where land prices were cheap. Leaping over the Palatine settlements, the Scots-Irish filled the hilly country along the western fringes of the Susquehanna Valley, then turned southward to engulf the southern Shenandoah country and especially the valley lands south of the James River. There, on the extreme edge of civilization, they learned the frontier techniques that equipped them to lead the march into the trans-Appalachian region a generation later.

Settlement of the New England Upcountry. While southerners and newcomers converged on the Virginia and Carolina backcountry, New Englanders during the early years of the eighteenth century were spreading over the hilly uplands that had been neglected in the past: the central plateaus, the Berkshire regions of Massachusetts and Connecticut, and the inter-mountain valleys of Maine, New Hampshire, and Vermont. The pioneers into this portion of the Old West came largely from the coastal and river lowlands, where Puritan fathers proved more fertile than their lands; they engulfed the hill-country between the sea and the Connecticut River first, then turned northward to overrun the rugged country that bordered Massachusetts. Between 1760 and 1776 seventy-four towns were settled in Vermont, one hundred in New Hampshire, and ninety-four in Maine.

The volume of this migration wrought a revolution in New England's frontier process. Town proprietors pledged to allot land free to orthodox newcomers became more and more reluctant to do so as they scented the chance of future profits from its sale, while even the legislatures succumbed to the speculative spirit. Connecticut began auctioning off town-sites in 1715 rather than giving them to proprietors; Massachusetts took its first step in the same direction in 1727 by laying out nine towns for soldiers who had fought in King Philip's War, then in the 1740's started selling land openly. Thus did the acquisitive instinct, so usual on all frontiers, disrupt the functioning of even such a well-disciplined institution as the Puritan Church.

East-West Conflicts. The occupation of the Old West boded ill for colonial harmony, for the social order evolving there, blended from the divergent cultures represented among the pioneers and altered by the forest environment, was fundamentally different from that of the East. Men in the backwoods dressed in a mixture of animal skins and homespuns, lived in skillfully fashioned log cabins, and judged the worth of their fellows by the skills that were shown with the ax and the long rifle rather than in terms of wealth or hereditary privileges. (See Document No. 2.) Whether they lived beside the rippling Yadkin River in the Carolina's or beneath the long shadows of Vermont's Green Mountains, they were arrogantly aware of their ability to tame stubborn nature and hence sure of their superiority over the rest of mankind. Democratic, poverty-ridden, and infinitely proud,

the frontiersmen looked on easterners as grasping aristo-
crats whose control of the colonial legislatures threatened
the natural development of American civilization.

These antagonisms disrupted the harmony of every
colony and flared into open revolt in three. In Pennsylvania the frontiersmen, alarmed at the failure of the
Quaker legislature to protect them from Indian attacks,
in 1763 organized themselves as the Paxton Boys and
were only dissuaded from attacking Philadelphia by the
diplomatic skill of Benjamin Franklin. In the Carolinas
the results were more serious. There an aristocratic,
planter-dominated government that denied interior farmers both legal rights and a voice in affairs, and a corrupt
tax system that oppressed the poor, goaded them into
forming the "Regulation," an extra-legal body whose
members were pledged to pay no taxes until convinced
that the money was properly used. When the Regulators
were branded as treasonable, warfare followed in both
colonies. In South Carolina the embattled frontiersmen
were defeated by colonial militia at the Battle of Saluda
River (1769), and in North Carolina at the Battle of
the Alamance (1771). These sectional conflicts ended
with the westerners broken but unbowed, and the issues
that underlay their resistance still rankling.

Removal of the French Barrier.   Before the defeated
Regulators could retreat farther into the wilderness, the
trans-Appalachian country must be won by England. For
while the Anglo-American frontier had inched slowly
toward the mountains, the French conquest of America's
interior had been swift and spectacular. When England
awakened to its danger, France controlled not only Canada but the entire interior valley from the Gulf of Mexico
to Lake Superior. This vast hinterland must be won by
a century of war and diplomacy before the American advance could be resumed.

New France's mercurial expansion can be explained
by the accidents of geography. Her principal settlement,
Quebec, lay athwart two tempting water highways to
the interior—the St. Lawrence and Ottawa rivers. Why
bother to grub a living from the soil when easy access
to the fur-rich lands of mid-America beckoned? So Samuel
de Champlain had reasoned, and his blueprints for ex-

pansion became the model on which his successors built their empire. By the 1660's *voyageurs* were tapping the resources of the Lake Superior country; in the 1670's they reached the Mississippi River over portages from Lake Michigan; within three decades thereafter they had scattered their trading posts over all that giant hinterland: at Niagara, Detroit, Mackinac, and Green Bay in the Great Lakes region, at Kaskaskia and Cahokia in the Illinois country, at the mouth of the Mississippi. When the English at the end of the seventeenth century became aware of this threat to their own expansion, war was inevitable.

Actually four titanic struggles were needed to settle the ownership of the Mississippi Valley. Three of these— King William's War (1689-1697), Queen Anne's War (1702-1713), and King George's War (1744-1748)— were fought largely in Europe and were indecisive; only the last, the Seven Years' War 1754-1763), was primarily an American conflict with results vital to the history of frontier expansion.

The chain of events leading to this struggle began in the 1730's and 1740's when the French pushed their frontier eastward by fortifying the Maumee River– Wabash River portage between Lake Erie and the Ohio River, just as fur traders from Pennsylvania extended their operations into the over-mountain area near the Forks of the Ohio. For a time the two trading frontiers clashed, with the French daily more aware that they would lose all unless they closed the West to the Pennsylvanians with their superior English-manufactured trading goods. This step was taken in 1753-1754 when work parties were sent to build a chain of forts along the French Creek-Allegheny River portage between Lake Erie and the Ohio. Knowing that the entire interior would be closed to them if this barrier was allowed to remain, the English countered by sending a small army against the most important fortification, Fort Duquesne at the Forks of the Ohio, in 1754. The clash in the Pennsylvania backwoods that followed touched off the Seven Years' War.

For a time the French and their Indian allies threatened not only to hold the interior but to wrest even the coastal colonies from the inept British generals sent to defend them, but the tide of battle turned in 1757 when William

Pitt became prime minister. Firing his countrymen with his own energy and vision, he placed his armies under brilliant young generals elevated from the ranks and sent them forth to win a series of remarkable victories. Fort Duquesne fell to an army under General John Forbes in 1758; a year later the mighty fortress at Quebec capitulated before General James Wolfe after a bitter struggle that cost the British commander his life; when Montreal surrendered in 1760 the war was over in America. England's victories were recognized in the Treaty of Paris (1763), which awarded England both Canada and all North American lands east of the Mississippi. Spain, France's ally, was compensated for its loss of the Floridas with the French territory of Louisiana lying beyond that stream. Once more the road to the interior was opened to Anglo-American frontiersmen and the advance westward could be resumed.

— 3 —

SURMOUNTING THE APPALACHIAN BARRIER, 1763–1812

Frontiersmen hoping to sweep across the Appalachians into Britain's new-won lands found their path still blocked in 1763. Guarding the gates now were English statesmen, fearful that an uncontrolled migration would goad the Indians into warfare or end the thriving fur trade in which many were personally interested. During the next years these officials labored mightily but in vain to devise a western policy that would allow the orderly settlement of the West while protecting the divergent groups with eco-

nomic interests there. In the end they failed, for nothing
could hold back the pioneer when good lands lay ahead.

British Western Policy. Scarcely had England begun to fashion a western policy when Pontiac's Rebellion
(1763-1764), a bloody Indian uprising that almost succeeded in retaking the entire over-mountain country for
the red men (see Document No. 3), forced immediate
action. The hurriedly drafted Proclamation of 1763 for-
bade settlement west of a line drawn down the crest of
the Appalachians, at the same time opening the new colonies of Canada, East Florida, and West Florida to frontiersmen. A year later the Plan of 1764 provided for an
elaborate system of controls over the fur trade. Angry
Americans concluded that the expansionist dreams were
being sacrificed for the benefit of the despised natives.

Their pressure would have doomed these regulatory
measures eventually, but the demise was hurried by the
opposition of a smaller but more influential group: the
land speculators. Even before 1763 land-jobbers, sensing
the fabulous profits waiting those who could pre-empt the
West before the rush there began, had begun to organize
to win grants from the crown; now their agents swarmed
over London to buttonhole cabinet ministers and members
of Parliament. Three companies were especially insistent:
the Ohio Company of Virginia which sought lands south
of the Forks of the Ohio, the Illinois Company of Pennsylvania and New Jersey which petitioned for a tract along
the Wabash River, and the Indiana Company of Pennsylvania which was determined to secure the same region
coveted by the Ohio Company.

Speculators won their first victory in 1768 when colonial agents were ordered to draft Indian treaties that
would shift the demarcation line westward. The most
important of these, the Treaty of Fort Stanwix, opened
most of western Pennsylvania and Virginia to settlement,
but more important was their effect on the frontiersmen.
Clearly Britain's restraining measures could be removed
whenever pressure was great enough; in effect the western
policy was worthless and could be ignored. As they happily awakened to this realization, Americans began moving into the West once more, flagrantly disregarding every
effort to stop them.

Peopling the Upper Ohio Valley. The frontier line gave way first in Pennsylvania, Virginia, and North Carolina where the influx of Palatines and Scots-Irish had built up the greatest population pressures. Some frontiersmen surged forward over Forbes Road to build their cabins around the Forks of the Ohio and westward along that stream; by 1771 some 10,000 families occupied the region around Pittsburgh. Others ventured into the maze of streams that formed the headwaters of the Tennessee River, led by James Robertson who moved his family to the banks of the Watauga River in 1771. As population was swelled by the influx of disgruntled Regulators after the Battle of Alamance, the tiny outpost slowly developed an atmosphere of permanence with expanding fields and a compact—the Watauga Association—to provide for self-government until the regular law agencies could overtake them.

More dramatic was the movement into the Blue Grass region of Kentucky. Well advertised by the "long hunters" who began seeking deer skins there in the 1760's, Kentucky remained inaccessible to farmers lacking the stamina to scale the Appalachians until 1769 when the greatest of the hunters, Daniel Boone, discovered Cumberland Gap. This flaring portal through the mountain wall provided easy access to the interior, but settlers still hesitated to move so long as warring Cherokee and Shawnee bands roamed freely there, justifying the land's reputation as the "dark and bloody ground." In 1774, however, the Shawnee challenged Britain in the brief but decisive Lord Dunmore's War which cost them the right to hunt south of the Ohio River. Now only the Cherokee claimed Kentucky, and negotiations with them might open the Blue Grass region to pioneers.

This was the dream of a wealthy North Carolina speculator, Judge Richard Henderson, when he formed the Transylvania Company and persuaded the Cherokee to sell him all of "Old Kaintuck" at the Treaty of Sycamore Shoals (1775). That the Indians had no legal right to sell under British law made no difference to Henderson; imperial controls were dissolving rapidly with the approach of the American Revolution and any lucky jobber actually in possession might make good his claim.

Even before the Cherokee chiefs had affixed their marks to the treaty, Judge Henderson sent Daniel Boone with thirty axmen to cut the Wilderness Road through the Cumberland Gap to the Blue Grass country. He followed a few days later, leading a band of settlers who were willing to risk Indian wrath and uncertain land titles to pioneer this newest frontier. (*See Document No. 4.*) Before they reached the Kentucky River, where Boone's men were throwing together the cluster of crude cabins they called Boonesborough, the individualism common among frontiersmen began to assert itself. Lustily proclaiming that the Transylvania Company had no right to the soil, a group under Benjamin Logan broke away to found their own outpost, St. Asaph's Station. Others followed to build a number of tiny settlements—Harrodsburg, Boiling Spring's Station, Leestown, and Martin's Station—nearby, most of them refusing to accept rule by the company. Eventually these rebels petitioned Virginia to organize the County of Kentucky, a step that ended Judge Henderson's last hope of securing any profit on his venture.

The West in the Revolution. Scarcely were the over-mountain settlements founded than they faced a danger that threatened their very existence, for the warfare that followed the drafting of the American Declaration of Independence in the spring of 1776 was certain to take a frightful toll there. The Indians saw to that. Bitterly resentful of the influx of land-hungry Americans, they were eager to ally with England in a desperate bid to drive the invaders back beyond the Appalachians, just as they had allied with the French a generation before for the same purpose. The English thoroughly disliked this alliance, for they were repelled by the cruelty of savage warfare, but they were powerless to restrain the red men.

The heaviest blows fell on Kentucky. As Shawnee and Delaware raiding parties crossed the Ohio with tomahawk and scalping knife in hand, the settlers fled eastward or took refuge in one of the three forts that resisted the attacks: Boonesborough, St. Asaph's, and Harrodsburg. By the winter of 1777-1778 these palisaded posts were under almost constant siege, with life within them so cramped and dismal that the demand for relief was swelling to threatening proportions. George Washington's armies were too busy in the East to heed the laments of the frontiersmen, but one of their own number, George Rogers Clark, took matters into his own hands. Securing a commission from the Virginia legislature, he led a band of recruits to take the British posts at Kaskaskia and Cahokia in the Illinois country, then with his flanks secure, moved against Vincennes as a necessary prelude to an attack on Detroit. After a march of unbelievable difficulty (February, 1779), Vincennes capitulated (*see Document No. 5*), but Clark's dream of capturing Detroit evaporated when needed recruits failed to appear.

On other frontiers a new aggressive spirit inspired by his success won the Americans a few precious victories during 1779; Indians and Tories who had been ravaging western New York were crushed by a force under General John Sullivan, while in the South an army of backwoodsmen under Colonel Evan Shelby nipped in the bud an uprising of Tennessee Indians. So strong was the expansionist spirit among frontiersmen that these few triumphs set in motion a new surge of population westward that lasted to the close of the war. Beginning in the fall of 1779 settlers began flocking into Kentucky and eastern Tennessee in such numbers that by 1783 some 20,000 lived there. Others, recruited largely from the Watauga settlements and led by James Robertson, opened a new frontier in the Nashville Basin of the Cumberland River which later evolved into the village of Nashville. Renewed Indian attacks took a heavy toll in these distant outposts, but the frontiersmen managed to cling to their lands until the treaty of peace ended fighting in 1783.

That document, the Treaty of Paris, assured the newborn United States not only independence but continued room for expansion. Yet favorable though it was in allotting the nation all lands westward to the Mississippi, the treaty created a number of problems that kept the West in a turmoil for a generation. The most troublesome of these concerned the southern boundary. The Floridas were returned to Spain, but a series of indefinite clauses convinced both that country and the United States that each owned a strip of land lying between the line of 32° 28′ and the 31st parallel. The controversy over that "Yazoo

Strip" was to cost the Southwest heavily in lives and money before it was settled in favor of the Americans more than a decade later.

American Western Policy. Pioneers who fondly believed that independence would open the West to their unrestrained exploitation were destined to be disappointed in 1783 as they had been in 1763, for the new government of the United States faced the identical problem that had confronted Britain's ministers a generation before: how could migration be controlled to assure both revenue from land sales and satisfaction for expansionist-minded frontiersmen on the one hand, and peace with the Indians on the other? England's best statesmen had failed to solve that problem after 1763; now an untried republic, torn by dissension and threatened by enemies, must succeed or witness the failure of its experiment in popular rule.

Before Congress could legislate for the West, control of that hinterland must be secured. At the beginning of the Revolution, all the trans-Appalachian country was claimed by seven of the states on the basis of their original charters which had contained sea-to-sea rights. A demand that these landed states cede their western holdings to the national government had been raised at once by the six landless states, with Maryland serving as their principal spokesmen. The public utterances of Maryland's statesmen stressed the benefits that all the nation would enjoy through the surrender of this territory to the nation, but their stirring phrases concealed an actual conflict between two groups of land speculators, one convinced that they could secure grants most easily from the states already in possession, and the other believing that the national Congress would be more generous. In the end the latter group triumphed by convincing Maryland to refuse to ratify the Articles of Confederation, the nation's first constitution, until the landed states ceded. Faced by a rising tide of popular resentment on the part of those who knew nothing of the selfish motives involved, Virginia finally agreed to cede in 1781, with the others falling into line over the next years. Thus did Congress come into possession of a giant domain lying between the Appalachians and the Mississippi, which was destined to serve as a source of revenue and a bond of union for generations to come.

Because money was the first need of the national government, Congress gave land sales a priority over other matters in developing its western policy. After a heated debate that revealed the division between southerners who wanted to settle as individuals and northerners desiring to move in groups, the Ordinance of 1785 was adopted. This monumental measure ordered the prior survey of the public domain into thirty-six-mile square townships which in turn would be divided into thirty-six numbered sections, each containing one square mile. Alternate townships would be sold at auction as a whole or in sections, to satisfy both groups and individuals, at a minimum price of one dollar an acre. Admirable as the orderly system of survey established in the Ordinance proved to be, the measure failed to satisfy frontiersmen who had neither money nor need for an entire section of 640 acres. Hence sales were disappointingly slow; at the first auctions in October, 1787, only $176,090 in depreciated currency was taken in.

When Congress, alarmed by these scant returns and desperate for money, decided to sell a few large plots to speculators, it inadvertently set in motion the chain of events that was to lead to the second monumental ordinance for the West: that creating a governmental machinery for the region. One of the speculating companies interested in obtaining a plot beyond the Appalachians, the Ohio Company of Massachusetts, let it be known that it would purchase some five million acres of land only if Congress provided for a governmental organization that would attract settlers. Dazzled by the prospect of such a large sale, and with many of its own members financially interested in the company, Congress responded by adopting the Ordinance of 1787, or the Northwest Ordinance. This decreed that the area north of the Ohio River and east of the Mississippi should be divided into from three to five territories. When these were but thinly occupied they would be ruled by a governor named by Congress, but when the population of any one reached 5,000 adult males it would be entitled to a legislature of its own and a non-voting delegate in Congress, and when 60,000 persons lived there it could apply for admission into the Union on terms of full equality with the other states. A measure so liberal that it assured full political privileges to those moving westward was certain to act as an inducement to migration.

Diplomatic Problems in the Northwest. Yet few responded, for while the national government could assure newcomers self-rule and secure land titles, it proved less successful in guaranteeing them safety for their lives and property. That this was the case was not surprising, for the Indians who menaced the pioneers in the West were only pawns in the hands of European powers anxious to expand their own holdings at the expense of the weak United States. Their machinations kept the frontiers in a turmoil for a generation before the troublesome diplomatic issues were finally settled and peace assured along the borderlands.

The villain in the Northwest was England. Despite the end of the Revolution, that country continued to occupy a number of posts south of the boundary—at Oswego, Niagara, Detroit, and Mackinac—partly because their abandonment would end a profitable traffic in furs, partly because British statesmen feared the outbreak of Indian warfare if troops were removed. To the Indians, and to a few unscrupulous English agents, this was assurance that the red men and the red coats would soon fight side by side against the land-stealing Americans. By the summer of 1789 younger warriors were beginning their attacks, and the Northwest faced a serious Indian war.

The first troops hurried westward to quell this uprising did more harm than good. In 1790 an army under the aging General Josiah Harmar suffered a humiliating defeat as it marched northward in the Ohio country; a year later the inept General Arthur St. Clair led a larger force into an ambush that cost him nearly one-third of his men. (*See Document No. 6.*) The elated natives, confident now of driving the "Long Knives" back across the Ohio, were further inspired when Britain ordered the construction of a new fort, Fort Miami, on the Maumee River in undisputed American territory. Realizing that another blunder would spell disaster, President George Washington placed the third army of invasion under the able General Anthony Wayne who trained his men carefully before launching his campaign. When he was ready to move in

1794 his well-equipped fighters had no difficulty in inflicting a decisive defeat on the red men in the Battle of Fallen Timbers, fought under the very guns of Fort Miami. The cowed Indians, realizing at last that their hopes of British aid were in vain, drifted away into the forest, their spirit broken. A year later Wayne gathered a few chiefs together to sign the Treaty of Greenville, surrendering most of southern Ohio to the United States. At the same time the British agreed in Jay's Treaty (1794) to give up the Northwest Posts by June 1, 1796. These triumphs ended tensions in the Northwest for a generation.

Diplomatic Conflicts in the Southwest. Troubles in the Southwest were more serious, for the antagonist there, Spain, had both a legal basis to its claims and a trump card to play. The conflict centered around ownership of the Yazoo Strip, which had been awarded to both nations in the treaties of 1783 that closed the Revolution, but the Spaniards had more grandiose plans in mind than merely securing this territory. If the frontiersmen of Kentucky and Tennessee could be made sufficiently dissatisfied with American rule, they reasoned, some might migrate to the Floridas or Louisiana, or all might secede to cast their lot with Spain. Proper use of her trump card —ownership of the mouth of the Mississippi—could bring this about, for the American westerners were dependent on the use of that stream to export their bulky agricultural produce. Closing the river to navigation would surely create such unrest among them that they would gladly desert to Spain's banner, winning for that country all the lower Mississippi Valley.

This well-conceived plot was launched in 1784 when the Mississippi was closed to American flatboats and a leading Creek Indian chief, Alexander McGillivray, encouraged to take to the warpath against the backcountry settlements. With their economy threatened and their homes ravaged, many Kentuckians were ready to listen when one of their leaders, James Wilkinson, began urging desertion to Spain, little realizing that this polished scoundrel was being paid by the Spaniards to preach just this message. For a time the "Spanish Conspiracy" blazed merrily as the fate of the Union hung in the balance, but in the end the realization that life under an absolutist monarch would prove more uncomfortable than one under a weak Congress carried the day. When President Washington finally persuaded Chief McGillivray to end the Creek Indian war by signing the Treaty of New York (1791) and the new Congress under the Constitution showed a willingness to admit western states into the Union, discontent slowly diminished. Kentucky became a state in 1792 and Tennessee four years later.

The Mississippi, however, was still closed to Americans, nor were Spain's designs on the lower valley any less ambitious than they had been before. This was shown in the early 1790's when a new governor at New Orleans revived Indian attacks and renewed the "Spanish Conspiracy" with a few unscrupulous Americans. In the end this flurry of intrigue did the United States more good than harm, for the Indian alliances soon collapsed while the frontiersmen showed little inclination to listen to plotters who urged them to raise the standard of rebellion or to migrate to Spanish provinces. Convinced by these signs that its frontier policy was a failure, Spain was the more ready to come to terms with the United States when war in Europe made peace abroad essential to its salvation. In the Treaty of San Lorenzo, or Pinckney's Treaty (1795), the Yazoo Strip was surrendered, the Mississippi opened to American navigation, and the westerners assured the right to deposit and transship theirs good at New Orleans without paying customs duties. As in the Northwest, the peace that descended on the Southwest after a generation of turmoil opened wide the gates to a new migration.

Occupation of the Trans-Appalachian Country. The result was the mightiest movement of peoples yet known in America's history. From New England, the Middle States, and the South they came, driven from their homelands by overcrowding, rising land prices, and mounting taxes, and seeking beyond the mountains a mecca where ambitious men could grow up with the country. Some filled Kentucky and Tennessee, or spilled over into the Southwest Territory after its creation in 1790; by 1800 some 300,000 persons were busily growing corn and tobacco in that fertile country. More dramatic was the rush into the hitherto unsettled regions of western New York and the Old Northwest.

This began when the Iroquois Indians, who had long reigned over the lands bordering the Mohawk River, were driven from New York at the close of the Revolution. The rich land of hills and valleys that they had occupied was not a part of the public domain, but was owned jointly by Massachusetts and New York under their colonial charters; because neither state wanted to wait for the slow returns that would accrue from sales to individual settlers, both decided to parcel out their holdings to large speculating concerns. The purchasers were powerful companies backed by European capital—the Holland Land Company, the Pulteney Estates, and others—which operated on the principle that buyers could be attracted by hurrying the coming of civilization to their lands. With this as their goal, and commanding limitless funds, the companies cleared streams and harbors, built roads, erected grist and saw mills, laid out model farms, founded villages, and even provided taverns, theaters, and race tracks. The settlers that responded to these lures came largely from New England, in such numbers that by 1812 western New York was passing beyond the frontier stage and northwestern Pennsylvania was filling rapidly.

More venturesome pioneers from New England and the Middle States moved ahead to begin the conquest of the lands north of the Ohio. The occupation of this region had begun in 1787-1788 when the Ohio Company, having secured the passage of the Northwest Ordinance, sent its settlers out to build the town of Marietta at the mouth of the Muskingum River. They were soon joined by others, some attracted by the advertising of John Cleves Symmes, a speculator who founded Cincinnati, others seeking government lands that had been surveyed under the Ordinance of 1785. These pioneers bore the brunt of Indian attack during the troubles of the early 1790's, but with the peace that followed Wayne's victory at the Battle of Fallen Timbers, the rush began again in such volume that by the end of the century the entire region opened by the Treaty of Greenville was filled. To the northward, on the shores of Lake Erie, another frontier took shape when the state of Connecticut sold lands reserved when it ceded its western holdings to the speculative Connecticut Land Company. In 1795 this concern laid out the village of Cleveland and opened its holdings to pioneers; five years later the "Western Reserve" contained 1,300 occupants, most of them clustered in villages that fringed Lake Erie's shores.

The peopling of the Ohio country led to a demand for self-government that was not satisfied when the region was granted a territorial legislature in 1798. For a time debate over where to draw the western boundary of the projected new state delayed action, but that problem was resolved in 1800 when the territorial delegate to Congress, William Henry Harrison, proposed the creation of Indiana Territory west of a line running northward from the mouth of the Kentucky River. The eastern portion, where most of the population was centered, now moved rapidly toward statehood. A constitutional convention met at Chillicothe in November, 1802 to draft a frame of government that showed the liberalizing influence of the frontier in its provisions for manhood suffrage and the vesting of virtually all power in the legislature. Ohio became a state in 1803 with portions of its northern wilderness still unsettled.

As this filled over the next years, the principal migratory stream swept on into Indiana Territory. By 1805 population was sufficient to justify a legislature; at the same time northern Indiana was set aside as Michigan Territory. When pioneers began building their homes on the lower Ohio River at Shawneetown and Fort Massac, Illinois Territory was created there in 1809. Three years later, when Illinois earned a legislature of its own, 13,000 persons lived in the territory, while Indiana boasted a population of 25,000 and Ohio 250,000. By this time, however, migration had slowed to a standstill. Once more the Indian war whoop rang through the forests of the Northwest as the frontiers receded before savage onslaughts; not until a new war had been fought and won could the advance westward be renewed.

— 4 —

THE MISSISSIPPI VALLEY FRONTIER, 1812–1840

The Indian war that temporarily halted the frontier advance into the Ohio Valley was typical of most similar conflicts in early American history: it began when the red men, driven backward for a generation by land-hungry pioneers, were finally goaded into striking back to preserve their hunting grounds, and it merged into a greater international struggle. This was the War of 1812, fought between England and the United States over the right of the latter to ship its goods to Europe during the Napoleonic Wars. Yet the section of the country most interested in shipping, the commercial Northeast, bitterly opposed the conflict, while the area seemingly least concerned with overseas commerce, the West, was most eager to fight. Why this apparent paradox?

Frontier Origins of the War of 1812. Westerners were convinced by 1812 that only a war with England would solve three of their pressing problems. One was the depression that had settled over the Ohio Valley after 1808. This was caused by the faulty marketing system which forced frontiersmen to sell their farm produce in New Orleans and import their manufactured goods by expensive wagon train from the East, but not a man among them but blamed England instead. If that country could be forced to open the sea lanes to Europe, they believed, their surpluses would be sold and prosperity return. Another was the need for lands into which to expand. A conflict with England would make both Canada and Spanish Florida fair game for American conquest; Florida was needed as an outlet for goods produced in the Southwest, while the over-running of Canada might convince the British to grant freedom of the seas to shipping in return for the restoration of a portion of its colony. Finally, the pioneers were sure that a fight with England was needed to end a serious Indian war that was raging along the borderlands.

Actually frontier greed rather than British intrigue had touched off this conflict. Ever since William Henry Harrison had become governor of Indiana Territory he had forced land-grabbing treaties on the Indians, dealing with fragments of tribes, or bribing a few chiefs into ceding the hunting grounds of many tribesmen. Alarmed by their shrinking territories, the red men found a leader in Chief Tecumseh, who began welding them into a confederation whose members were pledged to make no further cessions without the consent of all. When Harrison, blithely unaware of this threat, in 1809 cajoled two small tribes into surrendering another 3,000,000 acres of choice Indiana countryside, Tecumseh decided to make his stand. An attempt to occupy the cession, he warned, would be met by force. Harrison waited to make his challenge until the summer of 1811 when the Indian leader was visiting the South in quest of members for his confederation; with a thousand men he marched to the upper Wabash, stood off the red men in the Battle of Tippecanoe, and destroyed their village of Prophetstown.

The full-scale war that flamed with this aggression was, the West believed, entirely Britain's fault. Not a westerner but was sure that every red-skinned foe had been armed and inspired by English agents at Fort Malden, a post on the Canadian shore of the Detroit River. Only by wiping out that nest could peace be restored to the frontier. This was the message carried into Congress by the "War Hawks," the wild-eyed western and southern congressmen under Henry Clay of Kentucky who gained control of the House of Representatives during the winter of 1811-1812. Their pressure goaded the reluctant President James Madison into sending his war message to Congress, and on June 18, 1812, that body responded by declaring a state of war to exist between England and the United States.

The West in the War of 1812. Westerners who dreamed of destroying Fort Malden and over-running Canada in a few carefree months were destined to a rude awakening. An ill-prepared army sent against that post not only failed to penetrate enemy territory, but was pushed back to American soil where Detroit fell in August, 1812. Convinced now that no invasion of Canada could succeed so long as Lake Erie was controlled by Britain, President Madison delayed a further attack until a fleet could be built and launched. When this flotilla under Oliver Hazard Perry won the Battle of Lake Erie (September, 1813), an army under William Henry Harrison was waiting in northern Ohio to be ferried across the lake for its assault on Fort Malden. The British fled as the superior American force approached, but Harrison pursued them so relentlessly that they were forced to make a stand on the banks of the Thames River. The Battle of the Thames (October, 1813) ended with the enemy in full flight and Tecumseh and hundreds of his braves killed. This decisive engagement broke Indian power in the Northwest for a generation, just as had the battle of Fallen Timbers a quarter-century before.

While William Henry Harrison was gaining glory in the Northwest, Andrew Jackson was emerging as the frontier idol of the Southwest. His first great victory was won in March, 1814, when he led a thousand Tennessee militiamen against the Creek Indian village of Tohopeka at Horse Shoe Bend of the Tallapoosa River. Storming over a log barrier, the frontiersmen struck with such fury that the bodies of 800 warriors carpeted the field when the Battle of Horse Shoe Bend was over. In the Treaty of Fort Jackson (August, 1814), Jackson forced on the beaten remnants of the tribe an agreement to cede about half their hunting grounds to the United States. A year later the fiery commander won even greater plaudits by soundly defeating an invading British army at the very gates of the city of New Orleans. The Battle of New Orleans (January, 1815) cost the English 2,000 of their best fighting men while only six Americans were killed.

The Treaty of Ghent that closed the War of 1812 cast little glory on the United States, but it did solve the problems of the West for a generation to come. The Indians, soundly beaten at the Battles of the Thames and Horse Shoe Bend, were in no mood to resist as they were pushed aside to make room for expanding settlements over the next years, nor were the British able to aid them. Once more the frontiers stood wide open, and this time expansion was destined to go on until the entire Mississippi Valley had been occupied.

The Peopling of Southern Indiana and Illinois. When the War of 1812 ended, the settled portions of the United States resembled a giant triangle, its base along the Atlantic seaboard and its apex at the junction of the Ohio and Mississippi rivers. North of this lay the unsettled lands of the physiographic province known as the Lake Plains: northwestern Ohio, central and northern Indiana, most of Illinois, and all of Michigan and Wisconsin. To the south lay the virgin lands of the Gulf Plains: western Georgia, Alabama, and Mississippi. These two areas were to be inundated in the "Great Migration" that followed the war, until by 1840 both had been carved into states while the frontier had passed beyond the Mississippi into the eastern fringes of the Louisiana Territory, purchased from France in 1803.

Responsible for the surge of population into the southern Lake Plains were the attractiveness of the region to farmers and the ease with which they could secure lands there. Most of the Old Northwest had been over-run by giant ice sheets during the Glacial Age; these had leveled hills and pulverized the soil to create a veritable agrarian's paradise. Nature had added to these blessings by dotting the forested countryside with "oak openings" and prairies, some of them small, others such as the Grand Prairie of Illinois a giant ocean of grassland, but all easily placed under cultivation. These could be cheaply purchased, for the Land Acts of 1800 and 1804, passed by Congress in response to western pressure, allowed pioneers to buy as little as 160 acres at two dollars an acre by paying only one-quarter of the purchase price down. With the eighty dollars needed to buy a farm within the reach of the most indigent, the term "doing a land office business" entered the nation's vocabulary. Even when Congress in 1820 was forced to abandon the credit system, it lowered the price to $1.25 an acre and the amount purchasable to eighty acres. Good lands, easily secured, were the magnets that drew men westward.

Those responding between 1815 and 1830 came largely

from the South, where they had been expelled from the interior uplands or from Tennessee and Kentucky by the expanding plantation system. Traveling westward over the Wilderness Road, or drifting down the Ohio on flatboats, they first filled the river bottoms of streams emptying into the Ohio River, then spread out over the hilly country between. By 1830 their cleared fields extended northward to Indianapolis in Indiana and blanketed the southern third of Illinois. (*See Document No. 7.*) More spectacular was the push of population into the Driftless Area of northwestern Illinois and southwestern Wisconsin where the discovery of rich lead deposits touched off a typical mining rush. Between 1822 and 1830 nearly 10,000 miners entered the region, to transform such cities as Galena into roaring replicas of later mining camps, complete with dance halls, gambling dens, vigilance committees, and almost daily mayhem.

Occupation of the Northern Lake Plains. As lands along the Ohio River filled, the federal government anticipated the needs of its pioneers by clearing Indians from the northern portion of the Old Northwest. Beginning in 1825, tribe after tribe was forced to surrender its hunting grounds, accepting in return annuities or reservations beyond the Mississippi River. This ruthless program inspired the inevitable resistance, although the spirit of the red men was so broken that it never assumed serious proportions. Sauk and Fox tribesmen who had been driven from their tribal lands in the Rock River valley of Illinois returned in the spring of 1832 to plant corn, but despite their peaceful intentions a panic of fear swept over the backcountry. Driven ruthlessly northward by militiamen, the Indians tried to recross the Mississippi, only to be massacred as they did so; only 150 of the 1,000 red men survived that grim slaughter. Black Hawk's War taught the remaining Indians of the Northwest such an emphatic lesson that 2,000,000 acres of land were ceded during the next five years.

These plundered lands were occupied largely by pioneers from New England and the Middle States. The completion of the Erie Canal, an all-water route between Lake Erie and the Hudson River, explains this shift in the migration pattern. When the Erie was opened in 1825 farm produce grown in the fertile fields of Ohio flooded eastward to compete with the grain and meat produced in the northeastern states. The hilly lands there could not meet such competition; for a time farmers shifted to wool production but by the late 1830's sheep growing was invading the Ohio Valley and once more the competition proved ruinous. As the "rural decay" of the Northeast began, farmers by the thousands sold or abandoned their rocky hillsides and moved westward, traveling cheaply and safely to Buffalo on the Erie Canal, and then taking deck passage on a lake steamer to the site that pleased them. As they fanned out over the countryside they filled northern Indiana and Illinois and southern Michigan and Wisconsin, then crossed the Mississippi to begin the conquest of Iowa's lush prairies.

Michigan felt the impact of their coming first. By 1831 newcomers were arriving in such numbers that every building in the tiny hamlet of Detroit was crammed to overflowing and its mud streets were bustling with activities as wagons were purchased, supplies laid in, and preparations completed for the last stages of the journey. Some of the pioneers followed the Territorial Road westward toward Chicago in search of good lands; others turned northward to overrun the Saginaw and Grand River valleys. By 1837, when Michigan was ready for statehood, settlements filled the region as far north as a line extending through Saginaw and Grand Rapids.

Indiana fared less well, partly because its reputation as a swampland discouraged settlers but more because of the over-enthusiastic activity of speculators. Their interest in the state was aroused by a Connecticut business man, Henry L. Ellsworth, who was so impressed with the possibilities of the Indiana prairies while on a visit there that he not only bought thousands of acres for himself but persuaded a widening circle of friends to do likewise. By the early 1840's, as a result, hundreds of thousands of acres were held by jobbers whose asking price was from five to ten dollars an acre; settlers refused to pay such prices when they could push on to Illinois where good government land sold for $1.25. Hence central and northern Indiana remained sparsely settled until the 1850's when rising taxes forced the speculators to dispose of their holdings at more reasonable prices.

Illinois and Wisconsin, suffering no such handicaps, filled rapidly. Chicago, a primitive hamlet laid out in 1833, began booming two years later as the jumping-off spot for the stream of settlers bound for the interior. The Rock and Illinois River valleys filled first, then the forested lands nearby, and finally the smaller prairies that alternated with wooded lands in the northern two-thirds of the state. These were subdued only gradually, for frontiersmen accustomed to a forest environment avoided the grasslands until nothing else was available; the central portions of the giant Grand Prairie were not occupied until the middle 1850's. Many seeking more familiar lands for pioneering moved northward into Wisconsin where they met another stream of settlers flowing westward from such lake ports as Milwaukee. A little later these Yankee migrants were joined by thousands of recent arrivals from Germany and the Scandinavian countries, attracted by the cheap lands and the rolling countryside that reminded them of their homelands. When Wisconsin became a state in 1848 almost one-third of its 305,000 inhabitants were foreign born.

This was also the case in the tier of states evolving just beyond the Mississippi. Iowa was opened to settlers in 1833 when the federal government took advantage of the victory in the Black Hawk War to wrest a strip of land bordering the river from its Indian owners. The rush began at once, transforming the hamlets that sprang up at entry points—Dubuque, Davenport, Burlington, and Keokuk—into thriving communities overnight and continuing in such volume that a second large Indian purchase had to be made in 1837 and a third in 1842. So rapid was the settlement of Iowa that government surveyors were unable to keep up with the advancing frontier, forcing newcomers to "squat" on lands of their choice until surveys could be made. When speculators swarmed in to capitalize on this situation by outbidding the pioneers for their improved land at government auction, the squatters organized extra-legal bodies known as Claim Associations to protect their members' lands by threats and force. Nearly 100 of these associations were functioning by the time Iowa became a state in 1846. (*See Document No. 8.*) As Iowa filled, the forested lands of Minnesota were opened to settlement in 1837, but not until 1858 was that territory ready for statehood.

Opening the Southern Gulf Plains. As Yankees, southerners, and Teutons hurried the coming of civilization to the upper Mississippi Valley in the years after 1815, their counterparts were affecting a similar transformation in the Gulf Plains bordering the Gulf of Mexico —but with startlingly different results. For while the Old Northwest attracted small farmers bent on growing the diversified crops needed for self-sufficiency, the Old Southwest proved a mecca for plantation owners seeking rich soils where armies of slaves could produce bale after bale of snowy cotton for the textile mills of Old and New England. They came in such numbers that western Georgia, Alabama, and Mississippi were overrun between 1815 and 1840 and the tier of southern states beyond the Mississippi River thinly settled.

The demand for cotton lands began to mount after 1793 when Eli Whitney's invention of the cotton gin allowed planters to shift from tobacco to this vastly more profitable crop but did not reach flood tide until the Creek defeat at the Battle of Horse Shoe Bend revealed the weakness of the Indians' hold upon their tribal lands. Then the cry rose that the federal government must rid the Southwest of these troublesome occupants. President John Quincy Adams was the first to respond to this pressure; in 1825 he ordered his agents to negotiate a treaty with the Creeks of western Georgia that would force them to trade their hunting grounds for a reservation in modern Oklahoma. The Cherokee, a highly civilized tribe boasting a written language and a tribal constitution of their own, were made to follow shortly after Andrew Jackson became President in 1829. One by one the other tribal bands were forced into line until western Georgia's last red man sadly departed for the West.

The pattern of Indian removal perfected in Georgia was followed in Alabama, Mississippi, and Florida. In each case fragments of tribes were bribed into ceding lands belonging to all the Indians, then the treaty harshly enforced. The Alabama Creeks and Choctaw made an effort to resist, but their brave defiance only brought troops to the scene to "escort" them westward at bayonet point. By the end of the 1830's, only the Seminoles of Florida still remained in the South. Retreating into the Everglade swamps, they fought valiantly until 1842 when the last band was subdued. Like their fellow-tribesmen, they were assigned a reservation in the "Indian Territory" of Oklahoma.

Long before the last embittered red man began his trek westward, pioneers were moving into the lands that they vacated. Instead of being attracted from the Northeast, the Southeast, and Europe, as was the case in the Old Northwest, the frontiersmen who subdued the Gulf Plains came entirely from the South Atlantic states, and especially from the Carolinas and eastern Georgia. For this unusual migration pattern conditions in the Southeast were primarily responsible. There, soils had been worn thin by generations of one-crop planting, with fields devoted to tobacco or cotton year after year having no chance to renew their fertility. This was especially the case in the uplands, where heavy rains washed and gullied the hillsides until scarcely an acre remained fit for cultivation. When farmers, small planters, and their younger sons surveyed the debacle caused by soil exhaustion, and contrasted the sight with tales they had heard of the deep limestone soils waiting exploitation in Mississippi's "Black Belt," or of the rich red lands covering the gently rolling hills of central Alabama, they felt that they had every justification to move.

The Southern Migration Pattern. So move they did, with small farmers in the van, eager to follow the usual frontier practice of spying out good land, clearing away the underbrush and trees, building connecting cabins with a roofed living space between, and supplementing the usual corn crop with cotton as soon as the family's needs were cared for. When each pioneer community reached this stage it was likely to be visited by a planter from the East in search of good lands for exploitation. These wealthy individuals had such a heavy capital investment in slaves that they could not afford the risks of pioneering unproven soils; instead they waited until a new region was thoroughly tested before buying up several adjoining farms that could be welded into a plantation. With the site chosen, they returned east to bring out their families and workers. Travelers in the South reported a constant procession of their caravans wending westward through the forests, with the wife and children riding in a buggy, the household goods piled high on wagons, and long lines of slaves plodding on foot driving the herds of horses and cattle. Each plantation planted in the Southwest displaced a number of small farmers, who moved ahead to begin the process anew.

The dynamic nature of the cotton frontier meant that the Southwest would be settled rapidly. For a time after the War of 1812 the "Alabama Fever" raged, sending land sales skyrocketing to 2,278,045 acres a year by 1819 and the price of choice lands up to $30 an acre. By the time the Panic of 1819 temporarily slowed the westward movement, 200,000 persons lived in the Gulf Plains and half the nation's cotton was produced there. Statehood followed inevitably for Mississippi and Alabama, with the former entering the Union in 1817 and the latter two years later. Through the 1820's settlement progressed at a slower pace, but the booming prosperity of the 1830's allowed cotton-growers to reap a 35% return on their investments yearly and once more the population tide ran full. By 1840 the boundaries of the cotton kingdom had been marked out and all the Gulf Plains settled save the lowlands directly bordering the Mississippi River. These were occupied during the next decade when cooperative effort built the levees needed to hold back the yearly flood waters.

So persistent was the urge for cotton lands in the South that the westward-moving tide vaulted the Mississippi to spend itself in the country just beyond. Louisiana, with a sizeable population dating back to colonial days, became a state in 1812. Missouri was settled next, for it lay just beyond the first trans-Appalachian states to be filled, Kentucky and Tennessee. Frontiersmen began building their homes in the lower Missouri River valley soon after the War of 1812, with Boonsville and Franklin as their principal settlements; by 1820 their farms stretched for eighty miles along the Missouri and statehood was possible. Arkansas filled more slowly, but by

1819 enough people lived there to justify territorial status. Over the next years, migration continued steadily until a somewhat optimistic estimate placed the population at 70,000 in 1835, with statehood following the next year.

The social structure that evolved in the Gulf Plains differed radically from that emerging at the same time in the Lake Plains of the Northwest. Based on the principle that large-scale production garnered the greatest profits, the region's economic system was built on the plantation tilled by slave labor. Yet only a few favored areas were capable of sustaining such oversized economic units, just as relatively few men possessed the wealth or managerial skill to succeed as planters. The exalted minority blessed with these attributes, and fortunate enough to chance upon superior soils, necessarily comprised only a tiny segment of the total population; the great planters who owned as much as 1,000 acres of land and as many as fifty slaves never numbered more than 3% of the people, yet they dominated the social and political life of the South. Far below them were the 20% of the population classed as small planters who owned a few slaves and toiled endlessly beside them in the fields; still lower on the social scale were the yeomen farmers who owned no slaves and the poor whites who had been relegated to worthless soils wanted by no one else. Together they made up 77% of the population, a vast majority. Despite their miserable, culturally-barren lives, they were the staunchest defenders of the slave system, for all dreamed futilely of becoming great planters themselves when fortune smiled at last.

The differences between the social attitudes of these southern frontiersmen and those of their counterparts in the Old Northwest demonstrated the manner in which men's views were altered by the environment in which they lived. Two social orders had emerged from the pioneering process, yet one was dedicated to perpetuating an aristocratic society, rigid class divisions, and an inhuman labor system, the other to maintaining human equality, social mobility, and political democracy. The westward-moving frontier had spawned two civilizations, so antagonistic that the differences between them were to lead the nation into civil war.

— 5 —

OPENING THE FAR WEST, 1825–1846

As the Mississippi Valley filled with planters and farmers during the 1820's and 1830's, more restless frontiersmen were beginning the conquest of the Far West. In that gargantuan hinterland, where plains and mountains and deserts mingled to create an environment new to the forest-adjusted pioneers, a king's ransom in nature's wealth awaited the first exploiters: a fortune in beaver pelts, scarcely-hidden lodes of gold and silver, fertile valleys needing only man's magic touch to pour forth their bounties. So the first-comers to this land were not small farmers from adjacent agricultural areas seeking permanent homes but nomadic adventurers bent on skimming off the surface wealth before moving on. They came as explorers, fur traders, trappers, prospectors, merchants, and finally pioneer farmers, and as their restless energies carried them swiftly over the Far West, they blazed the trails that more permanent settlers would later use to reach the tempting lands that they discovered there.

Government Exploration of the Far West. The shock troops of expansion who ventured into the trans-Mississippi country found sizeable portions of the land already occupied by European peoples. In the Oregon country, lying beyond the Rocky Mountains, Britain's venerable fur-trading concern, the Hudson's Bay Company, was firmly planted with its headquarters at Fort Vancouver on the Columbia River. In the Southwest, the Spanish pioneers who guarded Mexico's northern provinces—California, Arizona, New Mexico, and Texas—blocked the westward path of frontiersmen from the United States. These outposts were but weakly held; less than 4,000 Spaniards were clustered about the mission stations or scattered over the ranches of California, only a handful of hardy souls living at Tubac and Tucson had survived the incessant Apache raids on Arizona, about 40,000 served as sheep-ranchers or farmers in the Rio Grande Valley of New Mexico, and no more than 4,000 ranchers and townsmen guarded the vastness of Texas. Nor did these few sentinels of the borderland have any deep loyalty to their own country, especially after 1821 when the achievement of Mexican independence plunged that misruled nation into an era of perennial revolution and perpetual chaos.

So long as the French-owned province of Louisiana served as a buffer state between the Spanish borderlands and the aggressive American frontiersmen, this handful of guardsmen were sufficient to protect Mexico's northern states, but in 1803 the United States purchased Louisiana in what has been described as the greatest real estate bargain in history. Now two differing frontier techniques were arrayed against each other. One, that which had evolved in the United States, gave free rein to the individual to exploit nature's wealth as he pleased; the other, that developed by Spanish-Mexican pioneers, subordinated the individual to the higher authority of church and state and regulated his activities in their interest. When the two frontiers eventually clashed, the outcome was never in doubt. American enterprise was destined to triumph over the indifferent Mexican defenders, and eventually add all the Southwest to the Union.

First on the scene were the government explorers sent westward by President Thomas Jefferson to investigate the land that he had just bought. Even before the Louisiana Purchase treaty was signed, Meriwether Lewis and William Clark, two experienced frontiersmen, were on their way to St. Louis, recruiting helpers as they went. In the spring of 1804, they and their forty-eight followers began worrying their way up the Missouri River in keelboats and canoes. The first winter was spent at the Mandan villages in modern North Dakota; a year later they followed Indian guides through passes in the northern Rockies, descended the Columbia River, and by mid-November, 1805, stood on the shores of the Pacific. When they returned to St. Louis in September, 1806, they brought with them not only a vast store of scientific knowledge but breath-taking tales of a fruitful land awaiting exploitation.

The other explorers dispatched westward by Jefferson and his successors saw fewer wonders. Thomas Freemen led a party along the Red River, but was turned back by Spanish troops during the summer of 1806 before he reached its source. Zebulon Montgomery Pike was no more fortunate when he set out that same summer to investigate the unknown region between the upper Red and Arkansas rivers. After wintering in the Rockies he blundered into a Spanish force on the upper Rio Grande and was deprived of all his papers and diaries before being unceremoniously dumped across the border. The War of 1812 ended exploration after Pike's unhappy experience; only after the nation returned to normal once more was Major Stephen H. Long sent to investigate the upper Arkansas, Canadian, and Red river valleys. Tramping through that countryside in 1820, he was so unimpressed with the barren lands that he saw that his widely publicized reports created the impression of a "Great American Desert" lying between the Mississippi and the Rockies. This ill-founded concept served as a deterrent to migration into the Great Plains province for many years.

Expansion of the Trading Frontier. Government explorers, with the sole exception of Lewis and Clark, saw scarcely a single foot of the West not already well known to frontiersmen. Wherever they went, they had been preceded by trappers and traders whose endless quest for profits and adventure carried them into every nook and cranny of the country long before the official exploring parties reached there. By spying out the best lands, blazing trails over the plains, discovering passes through the mountains, breaking down the self-sufficiency of the Indians, revealing the weakness of Mexico's hold on its northern provinces, and advertising the richness of the lands they saw, these unsung pioneers played an essential role in opening the region to settlement.

One group was lured westward by the prospect of bartering Yankee gimcracks for the silver and furs accumulated by the merchants of New Mexico's capital,

Santa Fé. This sleepy little village had been closed to American commerce under Spain's rigid mercantilistic system, but with Mexican independence its gates were thrown open at last. William Becknell made this happy discovery during the autumn of 1821 when a band of Mexican soldiers that he encountered while on a trading expedition to the Indians of the southern Rockies invited him to visit their city. When he returned to Missouri in 1822 with news of profits of several hundred per cent, the trail that he had blazed was soon crowded with Santa Fé traders. Each year thereafter a wagon train assembled at Franklin or Independence or Westport, Missouri, chose a captain and lieutenants to keep order, and started westward across the plains. (*See Document No. 9.*) The trail tested the stamina of men and beasts—to the Big Bend of the Arkansas River, along that stream to the Cimarron Crossing, over the heat-seared Cimarron desert, up the rugged heights of the southern Rockies —but the rewards were so great that the trade persisted until 1846 when it was closed by the Mexican War.

More important than the Santa Fé traders in opening the Far West to future settlers were the fur trappers. They began invading the northern Rocky Mountain country immediately after Lewis and Clark brought back news of plentiful beaver in the streams there, but the expenses of the long journey up the Missouri River, and the problem of coping with hostile Blackfeet Indians who roamed that land, soon convinced traders to look for another hunting ground. The fortunate individual who succeeded in this quest was William Henry Ashley, a Missouri business man and politician, who after several disastrous experiences on the upper Missouri, sent some of his trappers westward across the plains to search for a rumored river that Indians reported teeming with beaver. Starting late in 1823 with Jedediah Strong Smith in command, these hardy frontiersmen crossed the Rockies through South Pass and finally emerged on the Green River, which more than lived up to its rumored reputation. All unwittingly, Jed Smith had pioneered a route that was to be widened by the wheels of countless wagons carrying overland immigrants westward over the years to come.

To Ashley, however, immediate profits were the important thing as he hurried westward in 1824 to capitalize on the find made by his employees. On reaching the Green River early the next spring he unerringly devised the system that was to bring success to the fur trade for a generation. Sending his men out to trap beaver streams wherever they could be found, he ordered them to report with their catch at an agreed-upon spot a few weeks later. Thus was born the "rendezvous." Each year thereafter until the mid-1840's trappers roamed the deserts and mountains of the Far West, running their trap lines during the spring and fall hunt, and gathering each July at a designated spot where they met a pack caravan from St. Louis bearing coffee, sugar, knives, guns, ammunition, and similar items to be traded for the year's fur catch. The annual "rendezvous" was the only contact with civilization enjoyed by the "Mountain Men," as the traders loved to call themselves; after two weeks of wild dissipation in which they drank and gambled away their year's earnings, they stumbled away into the forest to begin again their perpetual hunt for untrapped beaver streams. (*See Document No. 10.*)

The era of the Mountain Men was short-lived, for intense competition between the companies that supplied the trappers with goods—the Rocky Mountain Fur Company organized by Jed Smith and a few partners who bought out Ashley's interests, and the American Fur Company under John Jacob Astor that entered the scene in the early 1830's—resulted in such over-trapping that by the 1840's the beaver were almost exterminated. By that time, however, the Mountain Men had played their role in history. In their endless search for virgin streams they had explored every foot of the Far West, bringing back tales to the Mississippi Valley of lush valleys and green pastures that quickened the urge to migrate in thousands of restless farmers there.

Propagandists of the Far West. So great were the obstacles and so vast the distances confronting those who might feel the impulse to follow the fur trappers' trails to the Pacific that the population tide could not begin to flow until still another group had publicized the Far West. They emerged in many forms during the 1830's.

Some were governmental spokesmen such as John Floyd of Virginia or Lewis F. Linn of Missouri who used their congressional offices to barrage their countrymen with demands to open the Oregon country to settlement, whether or not this meant war with England. Others were idealists comparable to Hall Jackson Kelley, a Massachusetts teacher and writer who flooded the land with pamphlets, speeches, and newspaper articles praising the riches of a West that he had never seen and urging its immediate occupation. Still others were novelists such as Richard Henry Dana whose *Two Years Before the Mast* described California as a veritable paradise that God obviously intended as part of the United States. Equally important in stirring interest in the West were the published letters of early settlers in California—men like John Marsh and John A. Sutter—who were eager to attract immigrants to purchase their surplus lands.

Yet the nation's concern for the lands beyond the Rockies could never have reached the point it did had not another group of propagandists, the missionaries, added their voices to the swelling chorus. Their interest in the West was aroused when the visit of four Oregon Indians to St. Louis in 1831, although actually impelled by curiosity only, was trumpeted by the *Christian Advocate and Journal* into a mission sent to ask that the "white man's Book of Heaven" be sent them. Heathen asking for conversion were novel enough to galvanize the churches into action.

The Methodists were first in the field when the Reverend Jason Lee with a small party reached the Oregon country late in 1834. There he was welcomed at Fort Vancouver by Dr. John McLoughlin, the chief factor of that Hudson's Bay Company post, who persuaded Lee to settle in the fertile Williamette Valley, just south of the Columbia River, rather than among the Indians north of that stream. His letters home, all glowing with enthusiasm for his work and the delightful countryside, encouraged others to follow. Two Presbyterians, Samuel Parker and Marcus Whitman, built their mission stations at Waiilatpu and Lapwai in the heart of the Indian country during 1835 and 1836, while a steady influx over the next few years added dozens of missionaries and their helpers to the growing American colony. All served as effective propaganda agents. Jason Lee, especially, never ceased to glorify the agricultural possibilities of the Willamette Valley in his letters, reports, and speeches made during money-raising tours through the "States." As they listened, thousands of farmers in the Mississippi Valley were convinced that the end of the rainbow lay in Oregon.

This was an exciting realization to a people anxious to be on the move—but with no place to go. For a generation now population had been thickening in the states fringing the Mississippi, yet just ahead lay a barrier that could not be penetrated. Hemming them in was the "Permanent Indian Frontier," a tier of reservations bordering Missouri and Arkansas set aside in perpetuity for tribes removed from east of the Mississippi. Beyond the Indian frontier lay the "Great American Desert," a treeless wasteland thought to be forever closed to farmers. For the restless and the discontented the only hope was to vault these obstacles and find homes in the far western valleys so temptingly described by propagandists. The result was a surge of population into Texas, the Oregon country, and California that eventually added those distant lands to the United States.

The Settlement of Texas. The fertile lands of east Texas provided the first attraction. In 1821 an enterprising Missourian with Spanish citizenship, Moses Austin, persuaded the Mexican government to allow him to settle 300 colonists in that under-peopled country. Austin died before he could fulfill the terms of his grant, but his son, Stephen F. Austin, arrived late in 1821 with 150 followers who were settled on the fertile bottom lands between the Colorado and Brazos rivers. For a time growth was slow, but when in 1823 Mexican officials confirmed the title and decreed that each newcomer be given a square league of land for only twelve and one-half cents an acre, the rush began. Why stay at home, where farms sold for $1.25 an acre and the economy staggered under the impact of the depression that began in 1819, when such opportunity lay ahead? So reasoned the 2,000 settlers who reached Austin's colony during the year following, to build their homes about its principal hamlet of San Felipe de Austin.

The success of this venture encouraged Mexico to open Texas on a wider scale. Laws passed in 1824 and 1825 opened the whole region to land agents, or *empresarios,* who were authorized to promise each family that they introduced a square league of farming and grazing land; the *empresario* was to be rewarded with 25,000 acres for each 100 families settled on his grant up to 800 families, but would forfeit his holdings unless at least 100 arrived within six years. Within a few months after these generous measures were adopted the map of Texas resembled a crazy-quilt of *empresarios'* holdings, with all advertising everywhere in the lower Mississippi Valley for the settlers that would allow them to live up to their pledges. Their promises of free farms attracted 10,000 Americans by 1830, all of them loyal to their homeland, and most of them truculently resentful of rule by Mexicans who were considered an inferior breed. (*See Document No. 11.*)

This attitude spelled trouble. Conflicts began to develop in the 1820's over Mexican interference with slavery and Protestantism, but did not reach a climax until 1830 when the government, justly alarmed at the refusal of the Americans to assimilate, banned further migration from the United States. Strident protests from *empresarios* soon forced a modification that allowed immigrants to be introduced until existing grants were filled, but the harm was done. Not a settler but was convinced now that he was at the mercy of a dictatorial government, or who did not dream longingly of freedom. Dissatisfaction was increased by Mexico's refusal to cater to their normal desire for self-rule, always strong among frontier peoples. Instead Texas was kept as part of the State of Coahuila-Texas with a legislature predominantly Mexican as the differences in population justified. Separate statehood would have satisfied the Texans—for a time at least—but without that concession their discontent mounted steadily.

Matters came to a head in 1834 when the president of the Republic, General Antonio de Santa Anna, engineered a bold coup to make himself a dictator by dissolving congress and abolishing the federal system in favor of a consolidated central government under his personal rule. As Mexicans and Americans alike voiced their resentment against this infringement of their liberties, Santa Anna started northward with an army to crush an incipient rebellion. Only then, on March 2, 1836, did the fifty-nine delegates who gathered at the little village of Washington issue a declaration of independence modeled on the one with which they were most familiar. Thus committed, they fought a series of delaying actions with the invading army (including one at the Alamo Mission in San Antonio that cost the lives of all 187 defenders) while General Sam Houston whipped a force into shape. These tactics proved effective; when the two armies finally met at the Battle of San Jacinto (April 21, 1836), that of Mexico was completely killed or captured, and Santa Anna himself taken prisoner. Independence had been won, and the Republic of Texas took its place among the nations of the world.

During the next ten years the new republic grew steadily to a population of 142,000 persons as it cast about for a solution to its basic problem. Perpetual independence was certainly not feasible unless additional territories extending to the Pacific were added; an exploratory step in this direction, designed to court New Mexico's allegiance by establishing trade relations with that province, ended disastrously in 1841 when the "Texan Santa Fé Expedition" was attacked by Mexican troops and its merchant-members hauled away to Mexico City lockups. This dampened the Texan's interest in expansion and turned them toward the only other solution to their problem: annexation by the United States. By the mid-1840's they were ready to return to the land of their birth whenever an invitation was extended.

The Overland Migrations to Oregon and California. The pattern of American conquest perfected in Texas—peaceful penetration followed by revolution and annexation—was soon to be followed with minor variations in Oregon and California. The overland migration that filled those distant lands with pioneers was inspired by the Panic of 1837. As a numbing economic paralysis slowed business throughout the Mississippi Valley during the next few years, the thoughts of the more adventurous turned more and more to the tempting stories of lush valleys beyond the Rockies that they had heard from trappers, propagandists, and missionaries. Why stay at home, where wheat sold for ten cents a bushel and bacon was so cheap that steamboats used it for fuel, when good fields could be had for the taking on the banks of the Willamette or Sacramento? Through the early 1840's the "Oregon Fever" and the "California Fever" raged through the Middle West as men sold their scant belongings, pooled their resources, and turned their trains of covered wagons toward the setting sun. (*See Document No. 12.*)

The first sizeable band to make the perilous journey gathered at Independence, Missouri, in the spring of 1841: sixty-nine men, women, and children, all so poverty-ridden that their total cash resources were less than $100. First with John Bartleson, then with the abler John Bidwell as their leaders, they marched westward along the Platte River, through South Pass, across the Green River, and northwestward to the Bear River valley. There the already under-numbered party divided, with about half continuing northward to the Hudson's Bay Company's Fort Hall on the Snake River and westward through the mountains to emerge at Jason Lee's mission in the Willamette Valley. The remainder under Bidwell blazed a more precarious route across the desert wastes of northern Nevada, along the Humboldt River, and over the dizzy heights of the Sierra Nevada Mountains to emerge at the ranch of John Marsh in the lower San Joaquin Valley. The California and Oregon trails had been pioneered; the road west was opened to a new generation of Americans.

They came in a steady stream during the next five years. In 1842 small companies under Dr. Elijah White, a missionary, and Lansford W. Hastings, a would-be promoter, reached Oregon where they were cordially received by Dr. McLoughlin and deflected southward into the Willamette Valley lands that his Hudson's Bay Company did not covet. In 1843 three additional parties made their way to California, but the Oregon country was the mecca for far more. No less than 1,000 "emigrants" and

1,800 cattle converged on Independence that spring to make the long trek to that distant goal. By the time they reached the Platte, tempers were so sharpened by the hardships of the trail that the party split in two, some moving ahead rapidly, others following more slowly with the cattle. The leader of the latter, Jesse Applegate, left a minor classic of frontier literature in his description of the journey, *A Day with the Cow Column.* (*See Document No. 13.*) During 1844 five smaller parties followed the Oregon and California trails, while in 1845 five more made California their objective and three the Oregon country. A year later some 1,350 persons reached Oregon and 300 California.

Among the latter was one party that added a tale of tragedy to the epic story of westward migration. Organized in Illinois by two brothers, Jacob and George Donner, this group experienced no unusual harships until it reached Fort Bridger, an outpost west of South Pass built by an old Mountain Man. There eighty-nine of the emigrants were persuaded to follow a new trail just opened by Lansford W. Hastings which would, he told them, shorten their journey by 300 miles. Turning southward, the Donners and their followers wasted a month finding a pass through the Wasatch Mountains, then gambled away still more precious time crossing the eighty-mile alkaline desert that lay south of the Great Salt Lake. By the time they reached the old trail along the Humbolt the scant grass had already withered away, with further delays resulting as draft animals grew so weak they could scarcely draw the wagons. Stark tragedy was the result, for the party began their assault on the Sierras as the grey clouds of winter already whirled about the mountain peaks. When they were still well below the summit they were trapped by a furious storm, with neither food nor shelter to protect them. A few survivors from a brave little band who volunteered to seek aid—the Forlorn Hope, it was called—finally reached the California settlements, but only after being reduced to cannibalism. When rescue parties finally reached the remainder, only forty-five of the eighty-nine who had started were alive.

Sacrifices such as these were not in vain, for by the

mid-1840's some 5,000 Americans lived in the Oregon country and about 1,000 in California. Although few in numbers they were compactly grouped about either Lee's Mission in the Willamette Valley or the fort built by an eccentric Swiss adventurer, John A. Sutter, on the lower Sacramento River. Thus concentrated, they were in a position to exchange grievances and foment discontent. All were rambunctiously aware of their American heritage and unalterably determined to dislike any rule save that of their beloved United States. Not a man among them but believed their flag was destined to follow them westward. Yet this meant trouble, for two other nations were certain to resist such a step.

One was England, whose claim to the Oregon country was fully as just as that of the United States. Both nations asserted their rights to the region on early exploration, and both were content to let future developments determine ultimate ownership; England was confident that her powerful Hudson's Bay Company would keep out all intruders while America was equally sure that the expansion of its pioneers would tip the scales in its direction. Thus assured, the two powers had in 1818 agreed on a treaty of joint occupation, opening the area to the traders and settlers of both. But the fact remained that Britain had been more successful in this race for empire, for its fur traders dominated the region north of the Columbia River and could never be dislodged save by force. Similarly the California lands on which Americans were settling were undisputably Mexico's, even though periodic rebellions there had weakened the hold of that country to the vanishing point. Neither the native Californians nor the Mexican government would stand quietly by while the United States extended its protection over Americans who had settled there. Here, as in the Oregon country, war seemed inevitable.

This the emigrants were willing to risk, for as their stake in society increased with the acquisition of property, so also did their demands for a stable government to protect their holdings. To their minds, only their native land could provide this. The Willamette Valley settlers made this clear when they met at Champoeg in July, 1843, to draft an "Organic law" for "Oregon Territory" that would prevail only "until such time as the United States of America extend their jurisdiction over us." The stage was set for a series of maneuvers that were destined to extend the boundaries of the American Republic to the Pacific.

— 6 —

THE CONQUEST OF THE FAR WEST, 1846–1865

The American people cast their lot for expansionism when they elected James K. Polk to the presidency in 1844. Until that time statesmen had hesitated to annex Texas or occupy Oregon lest war follow, but the popular mandate for Polk whose platform called for the "re-occupation of Oregon and the re-annexation of Texas" meant that these earlier doubts must be forgotten. Rising to the challenge, the President undertook to achieve America's "manifest destiny" so successfully that within four years not only Texas and Oregon but California and all the Southwest as well had been added to the United States. With the road to the Pacific lying open before them, the pioneers swarmed over these acquisitions during the next years to reveal hidden resources beyond their wildest dreams.

The Annexation of Texas. The Republic of Texas was the first ripe plum to fall. By the time of Polk's election the 142,000 citizens of that new-born nation were eager to cast their lot with their northern neighbor, as they daily revealed in newspaper comment and diplomatic messages, but the United States was not sure that it wanted them, fearful lest annexation foment a war with Mexico and fan the flames of sectional controversy. For some months, however, the tide of opinion had been slowly turning, due largely to the machinations of England. That country wanted Texas to remain independent, to provide its textile mills with raw cotton, its manufacturers with a tariff-free market, and its strategists with a valuable ally in case of an American war. British statesmen attempted to translate their ambitions into action in 1844 when they proposed a four-party treaty between England, France, Mexico, and Texas, with each power pledged to protect the territorial integrity of all others. This meddling arrangement never passed the planning stage, but news of Britain's intentions sent a wave of anger coursing across the United States. Better to grab Texas at once than wait until too late.

Polk had yet to be inaugurated when this turn of events shifted public opinion to favor annexation, but his predecessor, John Tyler, sensed the change immediately. Anxious to win the glory of adding Texas to the Union, yet knowing that northern antislavery votes would block the two-thirds majority needed for Senate ratification of a treaty, he proposed in January, 1845, that annexation be accomplished by joint resolution of both houses of Congress. The necessary majorities were easily achieved, and on March 1, 1845, Tyler signed the bill that made Texas a state.

The Oregon Settlement. Oregon was not long in following. When Polk was elected in 1844 with his fire-eating pledge to add the entire Northwest to the Union, American claims to the region actually in dispute were hardly impressive. This comprised the triangle of land between the 49th parallel and the Columbia River, for the United States had no real ambitions for the area of modern British Columbia while England had long since decided that the region south of the Columbia should go to its rival. Within this debatable land Britain's Hudson's Bay Company was firmly in control, with its principal post at Fort Vancouver on the north bank of the Columbia, a number of subsidiary posts scattered through the area, and several large farms tilled by nearly 1,000 permanent residents. Americans who lived in the Oregon country, on the other hand, were concentrated in the Willamette Valley, south of the disputed region. If possession was nine points of the law, the British had every right on their side in December, 1845, when President Polk asked Congress to abrogate the treaty of joint occupation and extend the laws of the United States over Oregon. War under these circumstances seemed certain.

Just as affairs approached a crisis, the Hudson's Bay Company miraculously cleared the air by shifting its headquarters from Fort Vancouver to Fort Victoria on Vancouver Island, thus revealing that it did not consider the disputed region essential to its operations and leaving the government free to settle on the 49th parallel boundary if it chose to do so. Responsible for this momentous decision was the realization that control of the mouth of the Columbia was not essential for domination of the interior, a change in men's styles in Europe that made the "beaver hat" suddenly unpopular and dropped the bottom from under fur prices, and especially the attitude of the 5,000 American pioneers who lived in the Willamette Valley. The company officials, knowing that these ferocious frontiersmen hated the Hudson's Bay Company as the principal obstacle standing between them and the extension of American rule, were afraid that they might come storming across the Columbia some night, burn Fort Vancouver to the ground, and destroy the £100,000 of goods stored there. This was a risk they could not afford to take.

With the abandonment of Fort Vancouver, the way was clear for a peaceful settlement, for England's rulers were in no mood to risk war over a few square miles of wilderness that were seemingly valuless. In this conciliatory mood they sent word to Polk that they were willing to settle on the 49th parallel boundary. Although a few jingoistic westerners in Congress were inclined to hold out for "All of Oregon or None," better sense prevailed, and on June 10, 1846, a treaty was signed. The pioneers who trekked westward over the Oregon trail had carried the United States another step nearer its "manifest destiny" of continental domination.

California's Bear Flag Revolt and the Mexican War. Now California alone remained outside the expanding orbit of the United States, and conditions there were ripe for a change. Ever since the Mexican Revolution of 1821 relations between the Californians and their mother country had steadily deteriorated, until Mexican authority was virtually non-existent and periodic revolutions had wrought a state of near anarchy. Many leading Mexican-Californians, despairing of securing orderly government from their present rulers, were talking openly of annexation by the United States as the only solution to their problems. A modicum of intrigue, properly directed, could easily add this land to the Union without a shot being fired.

So Polk realized when he entered the White House, but like his predecessors in office, he made a last vain effort to buy California before stooping to conspiracy. When Mexican officials refused even to receive his agent, John Slidell, he turned at once to the only course that would secure the rich prize. Thomas O. Larkin, the American consul at Monterey, was instructed against hasty action but secretly assured that California would be welcomed into the Union "if the people should desire to unite their destiny with ours." Larkin, taking this scarcely veiled hint for what it was worth, began at once to form a pro-annexation party among wealthy Mexican-Californians, working especially with the influential Mariano G. Vallejo, a leading rancher from Sonoma. That his plotting would have succeeded can scarcely be questioned. Before it could bear fruit, however, his well-laid plans were upset by California's "man of mystery," John C. Frémont.

Frémont was already famed as an explorer when, in the spring of 1845, he led a government-financed expedition out of St. Louis to blaze a new trail to Oregon and California. When he reached Monterey the presence of his sixty ferociously bearded frontier followers so alarmed the Mexican officials that the party was ordered to leave. Starting northward along the Sacramento River, the Americans had not left Mexico's territory when Frémont abruptly ordered a return, probably because he had heard that the thousand settlers grouped about Sutter's Fort were growing more and more restive and might be goaded into rebellion with proper leadership. The opportunity to become a new Sam Houston was too tempting to resist; hurrying back to the lower Sacramento Valley he camped near the fort to await developments. These were not long in coming. Encouraged by the presence of Frémont's formidable followers, some of the more lawless among the American settlers decided to take matters into their own hands. Early in June, 1846, a band of them captured 200 horses belonging to the government, then swooped down on the town of Sonoma where Larkin's ally, Mariano Vallejo, was routed from bed and imprisoned. (*See Document No. 14.*) Having gone too far to turn back, the rebels raised a flag bearing the image of a bear over the Sonoma plaza and proclaimed California to be an independent republic. Frémont, entering into the spirit of the affair, set out at once for Monterey at the head of a boisterous army of Bear Flaggers and frontiersmen.

Once there, they learned that their own pint-sized rebellion had merged into a larger conflict: the Mexican War. Frontier expansion had made this unfortunate clash of arms inevitable, for as Americans overran Mexico and threatened to repeat the process in California, Mexicans realized that they must resist or endure the dismemberment of their nation. Nor was the United States without its grievances, for Mexico's failure to live up to its international obligations or compensate Americans for the loss of lives and property destroyed during its frequent revolutions justified retaliation in the eyes of many impartial observers. Both sides were convinced that war was desirable when Congress, on May 10, 1846, responded to Polk's fevered message by authorizing a resort to arms.

The conflict that followed was short and, for the United States, singularly sweet. An army under General Zachary Taylor, already poised on the Texas-Mexico border when fighting began, advanced to Monterrey and Buena Vista to defeat the flower of Mexico's army under General Antonio de Santa Anna, then settled down to await the enemy's capitulation. At the same time another force, the "Army of the West" under General Stephen W. Kearny, moved out along the Santa Fé trail to subdue the coveted Mexican "northern provinces." When New Mexico surrendered without a shot being fired, Kearny left some of his men to guard the new acquisition while pressing on with the remainder to repeat the process in California. Even before he arrived, that province had been won by Bear Flaggers and a naval force under Commodore

Robert F. Stockton. There remained only the task of convincing Mexico that it was already defeated; this was accomplished by an invading force under General Winfield Scott which landed at Vera Cruz and fought its way into Mexico City by September, 1847. In the Treaty of Guadalupe Hidalgo (February, 1848), the Mexicans ceded to the United States all territory north of the Rio Grande and Gila rivers in return for a token payment of $15,000,000.

The Utah Frontier.   The Oregon settlement and the Mexican War opened a new era in the history of the frontier. With lives, property, and land titles in the Far West now safe for the first time, the trickle of migration that had coursed westward during the early 1840's was suddenly swelled to flood proportions. Yet a peculiar twist of fate decreed that the first comers into America's new empire should not be adventurers seeking their fortunes but a band of religious zealots in quest of isolation from the persecutions of their fellow men. Their search led them to one of the West's most inhospitable areas, the desert lands of Utah, where they reared a frontier society virtually unique in the annals of the United States.

Mistreatment had been the lot of members of the Church of Jesus Christ of Latter Day Saints, or Mormons, since their prophet, Joseph Smith, founded the church in New York in 1830. Living briefly in Ohio and Missouri, they had known neither peace nor prosperity until they settled at Nauvoo in Illinois under their prophet's guidance. Nor was this haven to prove inviolable, for when Joseph Smith's revelation decreeing polygamy divided the Mormons into quarreling factions, their enemies swooped down to bring martyrdom to Joseph and his brother, and to send the Saints on their wanderings once more. Their new-chosen leader, Brigham Young, recognizing that they could know peace only by leaving the settlements far behind, led the way westward across Iowa during 1846 toward a destination unknown even to him. By the fall of that year some 15,000 Mormons were camped at Winter Quarters, a temporary village on the western banks of the Missouri River near the site of modern Omaha.

All that winter of 1846-1847 Brigham Young trained his people in the techniques of overland travel while he pored over travel accounts or guide books to determine their destination. When, in the spring of 1847, he led a "Pioneer Band" of 143 Saints out of Winter Quarters they were bound for the shores of the Great Salt Lake, the most inaccessible spot in all the West. The sun-baked desolation that greeted them when they reached their new home hardly gladdened the hearts of the Mormons, but with supreme faith in the divine guidance provided through Brigham Young they diverted streams gushing from the Wasatch Mountains to flood the parched fields, plowed, and planted corn to feed the 1,800 Saints destined to reach the desert Zion that year. Food was woefully inadequate during that grim winter, and for some time to come, but as a steady influx of new settlers poured in the Mormons gradually evolved a frontier technique suitable to their unique situation.

This was based on the sensible concept that a hostile desert environment could be conquered only by cooperative effort, rather than by the unplanned individual enterprise usual in pioneer communities. Land was carefully divided, with each settler receiving only the amount that he could till most efficiently. Irrigation ditches to bring water from the Wasatch Mountains were dug by joint labor and the precious fluid alloted each farmer according to a rigid schedule that would do away with any waste. The spacious streets of Salt Lake City were laid out by community effort and plots assigned each family for its home and small garden. On all of these projects, and dozens like them, the people labored happily and without thought of personal gain, for they were content to obey the will of their church leaders unquestioningly and those leaders recognized that desert existence was possible only when the good of society was given precedence over the needs of the individual.

This benevolent theocracy, so ably administered by Brigham Young, attracted a steady stream of migrants over the next decades. From the East and from Europe they came, willing to endure the perils and hardships of the overland trail for the peace and security waiting them in Zion. As their numbers grew, the settlements spilled over the borders of Salt Lake City and new communities became necessary. These were carefully planned by

Young, who chose the site of each, and selected colonizers representing a combination of skills and experience to serve as pioneers. Expansion over Utah and into southern California took place with a minimum of suffering as the Mormons watched the fulfillment of their dream of a "State of Deseret" that would stretch from the southern Rockies to the Pacific. Congress upset their plans when it created Utah Territory in 1850, but Young continued to rule over his contented people for another generation.

The California Gold Rush. The isolation that the Mormons sought was first threatened and then destroyed by an unforseen event: the discovery of gold in a mill race being built for John A. Sutter on California's American River. For a time the find attracted little save local attention, but when President Polk devoted a portion of his Congressional message of December 5, 1848, to California mining the whole nation went suddenly, deliriously, mad. In the rush of the Forty-Niners that followed, the West received its first sizeable population influx and the last hope of the Mormons for isolation went glimmering.

Those who could afford the outrageous charges left at once on ships bound for Panama or around Cape Horn, but most of the gold seekers spent the winter gathering supplies, converting the family wagon into a "prairie schooner," and excitedly poring over the misinformation provided by dozens of guide books that had been hurried from the presses for the occasion. With the first hint of spring they were on their way, trundling out of Independence or St. Joseph or the other outfitting towns so close together that the lead team of one train was seldom more than a few hundred yards from the last wagon of the outfit ahead. Most followed the familiar California trail westward but a dozen other routes were pioneered by those seeking a shorter way, nearly all of them leading straight to disaster. The 55,000 Forty-Niners who reached the gold fields by the overland trails, and the 25,000 more who came by sea, had been well tested by the time they could trade their last belongings for a washing pan and begin "panning" for "dust." (*See Document No. 15.*)

What disappointments awaited them. The gold was there, locked in the westward-sloping foothills of the Sierra Nevada Mountains, but most was buried deep in quartz veins while the sites along streams where scant quantities were mixed with gravel had already been appropriated. But prospecting was more a disease than an avocation, and so most scattered through the mines, a few to make rich "strikes," but more to settle down to the cruelly hard work of washing out gold-bearing sand in crude "cradles" or the more efficient "long toms." (*See Document No. 16.*) Wherever deposits were found mining camps sprang up, glorified with such names as Whisky Bar, Humbug Creek, Jesus Maria, Jackass Gulch, and Red Dog, where the Forty Niners lived amidst squalid surroundings, suffered uncountable ills, and dreamed always of the comforts of their forsaken homes back in the "States." In each of these a semblance of order was maintained by a crudely democratic system of popular government that regulated the size and working of claims and meted out punishment to desperadoes who swarmed in to prey on the newly wealthy.

From this chaos order gradually emerged as newcomers continued to crowd the trails to California during 1850 and 1851. Disappointed miners settled down as farmers or merchants to cater to the needs of the gold-seekers, or drifted into the rapidly growing cities that sprang up at strategic points near the mines. Stability attracted eastern capital which was used to devise new mining methods: "sluice mining" to wash the metal from low-grade gravels, "coyoting" to tunnel down to deposits at bed rock, and especially "quartz mining" to seek the gold that was locked in veins of rock far below the surface. As shafts were sunk and "quartz mills" erected by the hundreds, California mining passed from the hands of sourdough prospectors into those of corporations whose owners sat in plush offices in San Francisco or New York. California, already a state in 1850, was passing beyond the frontier stage.

The Eastward Advance of the Mining Frontier. This transition unleashed thousands of would-be miners who had failed to find illusive fortune in California but were too deeply infected with the gold fever to settle down to work in a quartz mill or on a farm. With washing pan in hand and a grub stake strapped to the back of a mule, they set out in all directions to pan streams and chip away at rock outcroppings over most of the West. Whenever a rare strike was made a rush followed, until within a remarkably short time the mining frontier had swept across thousands of miles of mountains and deserts, leaving behind a residue of camps and villages that marked the beginning stages of civilization.

Some turned northward, to find some dust in the Columbia River but far more on the Fraser River of British Columbia where a major rush began in 1858, only to dwindle away when the mines proved disappointing. Frustrated prospectors, making their way back toward California and panning streams as they went, made a series of strikes on the tributaries of the Snake River, the Clearwater and the Salmon particularly. As mining camps multiplied there, and as farmers moved in to fatten on the fabulously high prices miners would pay for food, Idaho Territory was ready to take its place in the Union by 1863. Others continued their search in modern Montana where James and Granville Stuart "struck it rich" on Gold Creek in 1862. A year later even more fabulous finds in Alder Gulch attracted a major invasion that turned the mining camp of Virginia City into a metropolis of 4,000 souls within a few weeks. Montana was granted territorial status in 1864.

Far more spectacular were the finds of prospectors who moved from California into the Southwest at this same time. Some made their strikes amidst Arizona's stark mountains, but more important were the discoveries made in the Washoe country of Nevada. There, on the eastward slope of Mount Davidson, a few disappointed California gold-seekers had slaved for several years extracting dust from the bottoms of Gold Canyon and Six Mile Canyon with only a few dollars worth a day to reward them for their efforts. One of the miners, "Old Virginny" Finny, decided in the spring of 1859 to test some likely-looking gravel that he had noticed near the top of Gold Canyon. To his delight he struck rich pay dirt about ten feet below the surface. A few days later two of his friends, Peter O'Riley and Patrick McLaughlin, made a similar find in Six Mile Canyon. All unwittingly these drifters had stumbled on the richest find in history, the Comstock Lode— so named for a ne'er-do-well named Henry Comstock who talked his way into a share of the O'Riley-McLaughlin claim.

The rush that followed was one of the wildest and most unusual in history. The thousands upon thousands of Californians who poured across the Sierra Nevadas to lay out the camp of Virginia City and stake their claims over the entire area found no gold, for the only wealth was locked in the deep vein of crumbled quartz that the prospectors had discovered and every inch of that was immediately appropriated by a few shrewd promoters with both experience and capital. Even they could produce no wealth until tunneling and quartz-crushing machinery was brought in. So men spent their days trading "feet" in non-existent mines that would someday (they dreamed) produce fortunes, and their nights in wondering how to pay their grocery bills. (*See Document No. 17.*) Gradually this picture changed for the better as capital flowed in, shafts were sunk, and the happy discovery made that the Comstock Lode grew wider and richer far below the surface. By 1863 Virginia City was a booming metropolis of 15,000 souls, with an opera house, three theaters, restaurants that rivaled those of San Francisco, and ornate saloons where bearded miners could quaff champagne rather than the "tarantula juice" and "Tangle Leg Whisky" in which they had drowned their troubles only a few years before. Nevada became a state, somewhat prematurely, in 1864.

The Rush of the Fifty Niners. Nevada's spectacular evolution was duplicated, on a smaller but more permanent scale, in the Pike's Peak country of Colorado. Rumors of gold in the Rocky Mountain country had persisted for years before a Georgia miner with experience in California, William Green Russell, decided to prospect the region with a few friends in 1858. Gold was found in Cherry Creek and the upper South Platte, but the finds were so disappointing that the miners spent the winter of 1858-1859 surveying town lots in the "paper" city of Denver instead of prospecting, hoping that a "rush" the next spring would bring buyers for their property.

They had gauged the state of opinion well, for tales of "Pike's Peak gold" were already circulating through the Mississippi Valley, growing with every telling. Merchants and newspaper editors saw to that, for times were bad following the Panic of 1857, and outfitting would-be miners would be good for business. By the spring of 1859 one of the most fantastic rushes in mining history was under way, with every trail jammed by eager gold-seekers, most of them with neither knowledge, stamina, nor worldly goods needed to face life in a mining camp. Of the 100,000 men who started west, more than half turned back before reaching the Pike's Peak country and most of the remainder followed suit after one look at the pitiful returns from the cradles already in operation. As they plodded back eastward they loudly proclaimed the "rush of the Fifty Niners" the greatest humbug in history.

The few experienced prospectors who stayed on were wise enough to recognize the similarity between the Rockies and California's mother lode country, and to act accordingly. They were to be richly rewarded. John H. Gregory made the first important strike on Clear Creek, convincing even the most skeptical that gold was there and sending an army of miners swarming over the mountains to seek it. During 1859 and 1860 deposits were found in Boulder Canyon, in the waters of Tarryall and Fairplay creeks, and along the upper Arkansas River, with the usual rush following in each case. As capital flowed in to finance the sinking of shafts to the gold-bearing veins beneath the surface the mining camps evolved into permanent villages, and the demand for self-rule became so strident that Congress created the Territory of Colorado in 1861.

The miners, whether seeking illusive fortune amidst Arizona's shining deserts or on the rippling streams of the northern Rockies, had played a yeoman's part in opening the Far West. Wherever they went, they left behind a residue of camps that served as magnets for capital; this in turn attracted workers, farmers to feed those workers, merchants to supply the farmers, and the dozens of others needed to plant the seeds of civilization. By the 1860's, when this evolutionary process was nearing its end, most of the Far West beyond the Rocky Mountains was thinly settled. Only the Great Plains, America's last frontier, remained unoccupied.

Overland Staging. The miners themselves, however, were less impressed with their contributions to civilization than with civilization's failure to keep pace with their rapidly expanding settlements. The government, they insisted, owed them nothing less than a fast mail service that would keep them in touch with their families in the "States" no matter how remote their camps might be. Now could the rumbling wagon trains of the private firm of Russell, Majors & Waddell that supplied western mines and forts during the 1850's answer the need? Californians, especially, would be satisfied only with lightning-like stage coaches, carrying both mail and passengers, and operating day and night with relays of horses to bridge the vast distance between their frontier and the East. Congress was perfectly willing to provide the subsidy needed to maintain such a service, but the usual quarrel between North and South over the location of a route delayed action until 1857. Not until then was a bill squeezed through which dodged the sectional conflict by authorizing the Postmaster General to select any route he chose and promised the company carrying the mails $600,000 yearly in return for semiweekly service of less than twenty-five days.

Thus was born the Butterfield Overland Mail, a combination of seasoned stagecoachers who secured the coveted contract by promising to follow a southern route agreeable to the Tennessee-born Postmaster General. Less than a year of frantic preparation was needed to scatter way-stations along the 2,812 mile trail from Tipton, Missouri (the western terminus of the railroad), to San Francisco, each bossed by a ruffian glorified by the title of station-master who guarded the herd of half-tamed horses and mules and was prepared to disperse greasy pork, leaden bread, and lye-like coffee to passengers hardy enough for such fare. By mid-September, 1858, service could begin, with coaches pulling away from Tipton and San Francisco simultaneously for the wearisome journey across the continent. (*See Document No. 18.*) It continued over the next years as the volume of mail steadily increased and the number of passengers, capable of surviving twenty-five sleepless nights in a jolting coach, mounted constantly.

The round-about course followed by the Butterfield

Mail—the "ox-bow route" it was derisively labeled in the North—called a competitor into the field. In 1859 the well-established freighting firm of Russell, Majors & Waddell formed the Pike's Peak Express Company to run coaches between Leavenworth, Kansas, and Denver, then expanded its operations to include service to San Francisco over South Pass. The hard-headed managers of this firm fully realized that their venture would prove financially disastrous without a government subsidy; their hope was to demonstrate the superiority of the Central Route through South Pass and win the mail contract from Butterfield. This ambition led them to launch the "Pony Express" in 1860 for no other purpose than to publicize their route; fast riders carrying the mails between St. Joseph and San Francisco in less than ten days were certain to focus world attention on the company. In the end this venture proved fatal, for it cost so heavily that Russell, Majors & Waddell were on the verge of bankruptcy when the Civil War forced Congress to abandon the southern route. Instead of entrusting the mails to such a shaky concern, it simply shifted the Butterfield line northward. A short time later the Butterfield interests sold out to Ben Holladay, a free-plunging promoter who managed to build up a monopoly in western stagecoaching before he in turned disposed of his holdings to the express firm of Wells, Fargo & Company in 1866.

By this time the day of the stagecoach was drawing to a close. Already telegraph lines spanned the continent, carrying in seconds the messages that the pony express had taken days to deliver; already crews of workmen were laying the gleaming rails that would soon carry smoke-belching locomotives over the trails rutted by the covered wagons of the pioneers. The West was poised on the threshold of a new era, where man would adapt the machine to his conquest of nature and hurry the day when the frontier would be no more.

— 7 —

AMERICA'S LAST FRONTIER, 1865–1890

By the close of the Civil War only the vast domain between the tier of states bordering the Mississippi River and the Rocky Mountains remained unoccupied. For generations pioneers had vaulted this semiarid, interminable grassland for the more familiar lands that lay beyond, sensing that its unfamiliar environment posed problems that they were incapable of solving. How could crops be grown where rainfall was sufficient to support only sparse grass? Where could men obtain fuel, housing, and fencing when trees were lacking? How could crops be exported over sluggish streams that dwindled away entirely in dry weather? So long as good lands awaited exploitation elsewhere these troublesome questions need not be answered, but by 1865 the settlement of the continent had progressed so rapidly that only the Great Plains beckoned the pioneer. Thus challenged, frontiersmen devised two techniques for their conquest, one employing an economic enterprise suited to the environment, the other using manmade machines to override nature's obstacles.

The Coming of the Railroads. Neither of these techniques could succeed until better transportation facilities than those provided by stagecoach and wagon train allowed man to cope with the vast distances of the Great Plains. The railroad was the only answer. During the 1850's Congressmen agreed on both the feasibility and necessity of a transcontinental road, but they were unable to agree upon a route until the southern states left the Union. The act finally passed in 1862 provided for two companies, the Union Pacific to build west from Omaha and the Central Pacific east from California, each heavily subsidized with land grants and generous loans.

Construction began a year later with the Central Pacific pushing its track across the Sacramento Valley to the towering Sierras that were finally surmounted in 1867. At about the same time the Union Pacific construction crews were starting the climb into the Rockies. Both companies pushed their workers feverishly to complete as much track as possible and thus be eligible for the lavish government loans that were alloted on a mileage basis; the Central Pacific built 360 miles of road in 1868, the Union Pacific 425, as they winged across the intermontane province toward a meeting. Finally, in mid-May, 1869, they were joined at Promontory, Utah, as all the nation celebrated the driving of the golden spike that symbolized the bridging of the continent. (*See Document No. 19.*)

Nor did it have to wait long to celebrate again for, long before the first line was completed, work had begun on half a dozen others. One, the Kansas Pacific Railroad, was chartered in 1866 to build between Kansas City and Denver, with an extension to the Union Pacific tracks at Cheyenne. Another, the Atchison, Topeka & Santa Fé Railroad, was authorized in 1859 to connect Atchison, Kansas, with Santa Fé, New Mexico. For a time work was halted by the Panic of 1873, but Santa Fé was reached in 1879 and a year later rights were secured that allowed the line to build on to California. When Needles was reached in 1883, and a connection with the Southern Pacific Railroad was made into Los Angeles and San Francisco, a through line crossed the south for the first time. A second was shortly added when the Southern Pacific laid its own tracks across Texas and Louisiana to New Orleans.

Two lines were also projected and eventually completed in the North. The Northern Pacific Railroad, chartered in 1864 to unite Lake Superior with Portland, Oregon, was still far from completion in 1873 when the panic halted construction, but work was resumed in 1879 and four years later the tracks entered Portland. Still greater difficulties plagued the Great Northern Railroad, which was projected without a federal land grant, but Devil's Lake was reached in 1883 and Seattle in 1893. With no less than six lines connecting the Mississippi Valley with the Rocky Mountain country and the Pacific coast, and with smaller spur lines projecting on either side, virtually every nook and cranny of the Great Plains was accessible to the frontiersmen.

Outbreak of Indian Warfare, 1861-1867. The revolution in transportation which began with the opening of the overland trails and reached a climax with the coming of the railroads forced the federal government to change its Indian policy, and in so doing plunge the West into two decades of savage warfare. The first step in this direction had been taken in 1851 when the nomadic plains tribes were gathered at Fort Laramie and forced to accept treaties that assigned each a definite hunting ground. While ostensibly designed to stop intertribal warfare by ending disputes over land, the Fort Laramie treaties were intended to make the eventual removal of the red men easier, for now each tribe possessed a clearly defined territory that it could be forced to cede under pressure. During the rest of that decade several tribes were persuaded to leave their lands in Kansas and Nebraska in return for hunting grounds to the north or south, thus opening the central route to overland travel.

Not until the rush of the Fifty Niners to the Pike's Peak country did this manipulation of Indian territories by the government stir up trouble. Fearful lest the miners goad the red men into warfare, the United States in 1861 cajoled the Cheyenne and Arapaho into surrendering most of their tribal lands in eastern Colorado for a barren reservation on Sand Creek, an isolated tributary of the Arkansas River. The transition from a free-roaming nomadic life to starvation on a desolate reserve as wards of the government was greater than many of the warriors were willing to accept. Falling first on remote farmers and stagecoach stations, the Cheyenne and Arapaho waged war until the autumn of 1864 when most of them were ready to talk peace. After delivering their prisoners to the commander at the army's Fort Lyon, the Indians returned to Sand Creek convinced that hostilities were ended. There they were surprised in November, 1864, by a force of Colorado militiamen under Colonel J. M. Chivington. Paying no attention to the American and white flags raised by the red men, the Coloradians began an indiscriminate slaughter of men, women, and children that ended with 500 of the Indians dead on the battle field. (*See Document No. 20.*)

The brutality of the "Chivington Massacre" fanned the warlike spirit of the natives everywhere on the Great Plains and by so doing helped foment the next outbreak. This centered among the Sioux, whose tribal lands east of the Big Horn Mountains were usurped by the government when it began constructing the Powder River road between the Montana mines and the Platte River trails. Aroused by this invasion, the Sioux took to the warpath in 1865 so successfully that a year later an entire detachment under Captain W. J. Fetterman was wiped out and a number of army posts threatened. The fierceness of the Indian attack not only stopped construction of the Powder River road but sent the United States into a period of agonizing soul searching. Were these wars, with their terrible toll in lives and money, justified? Congress responded to the rising clamor by sending a "peace commission" westward in 1867 to investigate the whole Indian policy.

Plains warfare, the commissioners agreed after carefully probing the situation, was inevitable so long as red men and white were in constant contact; peace could be maintained only by placing the Indians on small reservations far removed from avaricious frontiersmen. This decision made, the commission set to work on a number of treaties with the plains tribes, forcing those in the north to accept reservations near the Black Hills or the northern Rockies, and those from the south to crowd into the Indian Territory of modern Oklahoma or onto scattered reserves in New Mexico and Arizona. By the end of 1868 all had been assigned lands. "We have now," wrote one of the negotiators, "selected and provided reservations for all. . . . All who cling to their old hunting-grounds are hostile and will remain so till killed off."

Removal of the Plains Indians, 1867-1890. To decree that 100,000 people should abandon one way of life for another was one thing; to force them to make that transition was quite another. So the United States discovered as tribe after tribe rebelled against treaties that meant the substitution of sedentary existence as wards of the government for the free-roaming joys of the buffalo hunt. In the South the Cheyenne, Arapaho, Comanche, Kiowa, and Apache warriors who took to the warpath in 1868 were hunted down by an army under General Philip H. Sheridan with such devastating thoroughness that a year later all were reported safe on their reservations. Again in 1874 the Indians rebelled, plunging the southern plains into the Red River War that ended in 1875 only after fourteen bloody engagements had been fought.

On the northern plains the Sioux and Cheyenne were the principal "hostiles." Chafing under the restrictions of life on their Black Hills reservation, a number of warriors began drifting back to their old hunting grounds beneath the shadows of the Big Horn Mountains. By the spring of 1876 the army had decided that force was necessary to drive them back and three columns of troops were sent to converge on the region, one containing the unit under General George A. Custer that was destined to gain immortality in the West's most famous battle. Moving in from the northeast, the commander of this column, General Alfred H. Terry, sent a small detachment under Custer to swing south of the principal Sioux camp on the Little Big Horn River while the main body approached from the north along the Big Horn. Foolishly disregarding his orders, which restricted him to scouting the Indians' position, Custer decided to attack. The result was the Battle of the Little Big Horn, or "Custer's Last Stand," that cost the lives of the dashing commander and 264 of his men. Victory did the Indians little good for they were soon driven back to the Black Hills by Terry's troops.

The Sioux War of 1875-1876 was the last major conflict fought on the plains although sporadic outbreaks continued for another fifteen years: the Chief Joseph raids of the Nez Percé of Oregon in 1877, the ravages of the Apache under Gerónimo that continued until 1885, and the Ghost Dance Wars of the Sioux in 1890. These isolated incidents only emphasized the fact that massive Indian resistance to their conquerors was no longer possible; the slaughter of the buffalo herds by legions of hunters who invaded the Great Plains with the coming of the railroads left them no alternative but to become wards of the government, as their only source of food, clothing, and shelter disappeared. Congress recognized the inevitable in 1887 when it enacted the Dawes Severalty Act providing for a division of reservation lands into farms to be assigned individual families. Gone now were the tribal organizations that had futilely resisted aggression for centuries; the red men must walk the white man's path, and this path led to assimilation with the conquerors.

The Origin of the Long Drives. Indian defeat opened the Great Plains to frontiersmen. First to capitalize on this opportunity were the cattlemen, who were quick to recognize that the province's unique environment was ideally suited to their distinctive economic enterprise. Lands there were free for the taking, for years must lapse before surveys of the gargantuan area could be completed. Pasturage was limitless, while neither trees nor fences would interfere with the movement of herds from one feeding ground to another as the grass wore thin. Access to eastern markets was readily available over the railroads that were yearly pushing westward across the plains. An enterprising rancher had only to lay his hands on a herd, pre-empt a favored spot where water and grass were adequate, and watch his animals multiply until he grew rich. These were the inducements that in a few brief years transformed the Great Plains into the most gigantic cattle kingdom in the world's history.

The nucleus of that kingdom lay in Texas, where cattle introduced by the early Spaniards had multiplied so rapidly that by 1865 some 5,000,000 roamed there, most of them "mavericks" who could be claimed by anyone caring to fix his brand. Although considered valueless in the past because of lack of markets, these hardy longhorns assumed a new importance when the first railroads began poking westward across Missouri and Kansas. Alert Texans knew that beeves sold in Chicago or Kansas City for thirty or forty dollars a head. Why not gather a few herds together, drive them north to the railheads, and ship them to market to capitalize on this amazing price differential? Thus was born the "long drive" to provide one of the most colorful chapters in the history of the cattle kingdom.

The first herds were started northward in March, 1866, each numbering about 1,000 head driven by a half-dozen cowboys under a "trail boss." Difficulties were many, for the Missouri Pacific Railroad at Sedalia, Missouri, was the objective and the trail led through wooded sections of the Ozarks where the animals became unmanageable, but several thousand head were delivered safely. A year later the terminus of the drive was shifted to Abilene, Kansas, a site selected by an Illinois meat dealer named Joseph M. McCoy on the Kansas Pacific Railroad which provided easy access to Chicago's packing plants. Under McCoy's prodding Abilene was turned into the first of the "cow towns," complete with loading chutes, hotels, and a dazzling glitter of saloons and gambling halls where cowboys could be relieved of their earnings after months on the dusty trail. Nearly 1,500,000 cattle were delivered there between 1868 and 1871 when the advancing farm frontier in Kansas forced another shift westward, this time to Ellsworth on the Santa Fé Railroad. Again in 1875 the trail was moved still farther west to Dodge City. In all, more than 4,000,000 head were driven over these trails, transforming the "cow towns" into models of unbridled corruption and showering fortunes on the lucky owners whose herds arrived when the price was right.

Rise and Decline of the Cattle Kingdom.   Romantic though the "long drives" were, they were economically unsound, for the beeves lost weight on the trail, tribes in the Indian Territory charged a heavy fee for the invasion of their lands, and the arrival of dozens of herds at once each spring so glutted the market that sellers were at the mercy of buyers. The obvious solution was to grow cattle nearer the railroads. As this realization dawned, more and more of the herds driven northward were used to stock the range rather than being sold at the "cow towns." The result was a phenomenally rapid spread of ranching over the entire Great Plains country. Western Texas and the panhandle region were carved into ranches first, with Kansas, Nebraska, and eastern Colorado following soon after. By the end of the 1860's the cattle frontier was sweeping into Wyoming where the first pasturing began in 1868, and into Montana where ranchers began appropriating eastern grasslands in 1871. Within the next few years the Dakota country was invaded, and by 1880 the cattle kingdom embraced the entire plains from the Rio

Grande to the Canadian border and from the farming lands of the Mississippi Valley to the slopes of the Rockies.

Life within this empire followed a set pattern that illustrated anew the ability of frontiersmen to adapt themselves and their institutions to unfamiliar situations. Because water was the chief essential in that semiarid land, the usual ranch was laid out along a stream and extended as far as the "divide" or highland separating that drainage basin from the next. Sometimes the rancher took out a homestead of 160 acres on which he built his cabin and corral; more often he simply appropriated a "range right" which was respected by his neighbors as completely as actual ownership. In most regions any violation of these rights was rendered not only unpopular but unhealthy by extra-legal bodies known as Live-Stock Associations to which all cattlemen belonged. These not only enforced each member's right to his ranch, even though he owned not a foot of the soil, but recorded brands and arranged the annual or semiannual "round ups" where cattle, that had drifted across the imaginary "range lines" separating the ranches, were cut out to be returned to their owners. (*See Document No. 21.*) As usual on frontiers that were well beyond the pale of the law, voluntary associations provided the cattle kingdom with all of the governmental machinery necessary to a smoothly functioning social order.

The efficiency of these organizations hurried the end of the range cattle industry, for the security and assured profits that they brought to the West soon led to dangerous over-stocking. As eastern and European capital poured in, and as adventurers from all the world hurried to seize the opportunity for sudden wealth, every last foot of grassland that could possibly be pastured was put into use during the early 1880's. So great was the demand for cattle to stock these burgeoning ranches that a Texas longhorn that sold for eight dollars in 1879 brought thirty-five dollars three years later and could be resold in Wyoming for sixty dollars. So much marginal and submarginal land was turned into pasture between 1880 and 1885 that only a favorable cycle of unusually wet years kept the business alive; when this was broken in 1886-1887 disaster struck with appalling suddenness. That summer was hot and dry, with grass withering everywhere and seasoned cattlemen selling their animals in panic rather than facing a winter with weakened herds. They were wise, for that was a winter long to be remembered on the plains. With deep snows burying the over-cropped pasturage and the thermometer recording temperatures of sixty-eight degrees below zero, the cattle drifted helplessly before constant gales until they dropped in their tracks or died by the thousands jammed in ravines. Their suffering spelled the end of the open range, for humanitarian sentiments as well as the desire for profits dictated that winter feeding must be the rule in the future. As ranchers fenced their fields and planted hay the West was converted from a land of drifting herds to one of well-tended pastures. The cattle kingdom was no more.

Opening the Farmers' Frontier. Even without the terrors of the winter of 1886-1887, the days of the open range were numbered for pressing in on the cattlemen from the east was the advancing frontier of small farms. Halted for a time by the unfamiliar environment of the Great Plains and by the practical difficulties of profitable agriculture in a region where the annual rainfall was little more than the twenty inches needed for normal farming, this frontier began inching forward once more in the late 1860's. Gaining momentum rapidly, it swept ahead with such swiftness that within two decades the whole region west to the 100th meridian had been placed under cultivation. This remarkable advance was made possible by mechanical inventions that reduced the difficulty of plains farming and by an effective propaganda campaign that convinced half the people of the world that the American West was the poor man's Eden.

The inventions followed naturally as the realization dawned that inventors solving the practical problems of living in a semiarid grassland—fuel, water, fencing, housing, and the like—would be fabulously rewarded. Joseph F. Glidden, an Illinois farmer and tinkerer, in 1874 solved one basic problem with the perfection of barbed-wire fencing; within six years 80,000,000 pounds of his product were sold annually in the West and the amount continued to multiply over the next decades. Equally essential was the improvement of windmills to the point that they could utilize the steadily blowing plains winds to raise subsurface water for livestock and irrigation. By 1879 a million dollars worth yearly were marketed in the West, although the high price discouraged their general use for another two decades. Farm machinery was also transformed to allow the mechanical cultivation of the large farms needed to sustain a family under semiarid conditions. Sulky gang plows that would turn several furrows at once, disk harrows to prepare the soil for planting, and grain drills that sewed seed from a battery of pipes were all in use by the middle 1870's. Harvesting was speeded with the invention of the cord binder in 1878, the header in the early 1880's, and the steam thresher with blower attachment at about the same time. By 1890 a single farmer could plant, care for, and harvest 135 acres of wheat, in contrast with the seven acres possible before these inventions.

Essential as these improvements were in the conquest of the Great Plains, they were no more important than the barrage of propaganda that turned the feet of thousands of fortune-seekers toward the West during the 1870's and 1880's. Much of this stemmed from popular misconceptions concerning the Homestead Act of 1862 which promised every actual settler on the public domain 160 acres free of charge. Actually this benevolent law, passed with the best of intentions, played an insignificant role in the settlement of the Far West, partly because a farm of 160 acres was too small to be profitably tilled on the semiarid plains, but more because speculators continued to usurp the best lands as they had through most of the history of the frontier. Some secured their holding from the railroads which had been granted 180,000,000 acres in the form of alternate sections on either side of their right of way to help them bear the cost of construction. Others purchased at bargain rates the lands alloted the states by the Morrill Land-Grant Act of 1862; under this measure every state was given 30,000 acres of western land for each of its representatives and senators as an endowment for mechanical and agricultural schools. Most sold to jobbers at once. Still other speculators bought up lands made available when Indian reservations were contracted, or hired armies of dummy "homesteaders" to stake out claims, or moved ahead of the surveying crews to pre-empt and buy thousands of acres at $1.25 an acre. In all they engrossed and sold some 521,000,000 acres of the West's best land, while only 80,000,000 acres were homesteaded. Newcomers unwilling to pay their high prices were forced to accept inferior sites far from transportation. Yet few men in America or Europe realized that seven or eight pioneers had to pay heavily for every one receiving a farm as a gift from the government. Instead the impression was general that all the West was free for the asking, and that the dispossessed could begin life anew there through the nation's generous bounty.

Scarcely less influential than the Homestead Act in publicizing the West were the land-grant railroads. Anxious to sell their large holdings as well as to build up traffic by scattering settlements along their rights of way, they all established Land Departments to peddle the generous grants given them by the United States and Bureaus of Immigration to lure prospective buyers to the Great Plains. The latter carried on vigorous campaigns for immigrants all over the western world, advertising widely through newspapers and posters, maintaining agents in foreign capitals and eastern ports to ease the migration, running free excursions to allow lands to be inspected, and in a thousand other ways using the arts of persuasion and overstatement to convince would-be buyers that the West was a land of milk and honey where the most poverty-stricken could become a millionaire overnight. The railroads' emphasis on Europe accounted for the fact that vast numbers of Old World aliens mingled with pioneers from the Mississippi Valley in pushing the farming frontier westward.

The Advance of the Farmers' Frontier.   This was the propaganda campaign that touched off the mightiest mass movement of peoples in the history of the frontier. Between 1870 and 1890 the Great Plains province was occupied westward to the 100th meridian where a lack of the twenty-inch rainfall needed for normal agriculture slowed the advance; in those two decades 430,000,000 acres were appropriated and 225,000,000 placed under cultivation. By the time the tide had run its course, the continent was occupied and the frontier closing.

When the movement began, the tier of states bordering the Mississippi River had been occupied and fringes of settlement pushed into eastern Nebraska and Kansas. Beyond lay the interminable grasslands where buffalo herds roamed unmolested and Indians hunted as they had for generations. The first intruders were farmers who moved westward with the advancing railroads, buying land near the tracks where they could be assured of transportation for their produce. One column followed the Union Pacific across Nebraska; two others hugged the rights of way of the Kansas Pacific and Santa Fé railroads in Kansas, especially after 1875 when the Red River War temporarily ended Indian opposition in the Southwest. As far as the 100th meridian they advanced, and slightly beyond for these were unusually wet years, then spread out over the intervening countryside less convenient to transportation. By 1880 Kansas and Nebraska were fully settled, with 850,000 pioneers living in the former state and 450,000 in the latter.

By this time another stream was swinging northward into the Dakota Territory. The first "Dakota Boom" began in 1868 when the Sioux Indians were concentrated in their Black Hills reservation and only ended in 1873 when the panic ushered in an era of hard times; during those five years thousands upon thousands of frontiersmen followed the railroads westward to break the prairie sod over all the countryside from Yankton and Pierre to Fargo and Grand Forks. (*See Document No. 22.*) With the return of prosperity by 1878 the second "Dakota Boom" began, stimulated by the vigorous campaigns of the Great Northern and Northern Pacific railroads for settlers. By 1885 all of Dakota Territory east of the Missouri River was occupied by 550,000 persons—a 400% increase in five years. Smaller numbers moved on into eastern Wyoming and Montana, to drive the cattlemen back as they irrigated the lands fringing the Big Horn Mountains or brought occasional watered valleys into cultivation. Wyoming counted only 62,255 settlers in 1890, and Montana 132,000. The Dakotas, Montana,

Washington, Wyoming, and Idaho were all admitted as states in 1889 or 1890.

The flood of population over the central and northern Great Plains left only one region unoccupied: the Indian Territory, or Oklahoma as it is known today. There lived twenty-two tribes, assembled from east of the Mississippi and all the southern plains by the federal government with the assurance that their reservations would be unmolested for all time to come. These promises meant nothing to frontiersmen as they watched the area of cheap lands shrink rapidly with the influx of population. Why should this garden spot of the world be wasted on indolent savages who could neither appreciate its beauty nor capitalize upon its riches? Why should the march of civilization be halted by a few treaty pledges with a barbarian people too weak to resist their violation? These were the questions being asked everywhere in the West by the early 1880's as orators and newspaper editors and politicans unanimously demanded that this untouched Eden be opened at once to men who could use it most effectively.

As pressure mounted, so also did the activity of a handful of lawless frontiersmen who determined to live in the Indian Territory whether the government liked it or not. Their objective was the "Oklahoma District," a 2,000,000 acre triangle in the heart of the territory that was not actually owned by any tribe. Beginning about 1880 bands of these "Boomers" under their chosen leader, David L. Payne, began a systematic assault on the district, moving in from every direction to mark out their claims, build their cabins, and defy the troops sent to drive them out. In vain were more soldiers hurried to the scene; for every Boomer evicted a dozen returned in his place, especially after 1883 when they organized as the Oklahoma Colony with all members pledged to defy every authority until their goal was attained. Such determination only whetted western sympathy for the Boomers, and intensified the demand that the government act. By 1889 this pressure was too strong to be denied; that year Congress authorized the opening of the Oklahoma District under the Homestead Act and on March 23 the President formally announced that just one month later, at noon on April 22, 1889, settlers could enter.

The next four weeks witnessed one of the wildest rushes in the history of the frontier as all roads leading to Oklahoma were jammed with eager homeseekers, each bent on obtaining a part of this last unsettled paradise. (*See Document No. 23.*) By April 22 some 100,000 of them lined the borders of the district where they played a constant game of hide-and-seek with soldiers assigned to keep back "Sooners," or illegal early entrys. Exactly at noon that day guns were fired, bugles blown, and pandemonium broke loose. Men on horseback, men on foot, men in wagons, all raced madly forward amidst a bedlam of shouts and dust and confusion to secure one of the plots available. Within a few hours the entire district was settled; by nightfall the tent cities of Oklahoma City and Guthrie were complete with streets, business sites, and populations of ten and fifteen thousand persons. (*See Document No. 24.*) A year later Congress created Oklahoma Territory, while over the next years reservation after reservation was opened as the principles of the Dawes Severalty Act were applied to force the Indians into farming and relieve them of their tribal lands. Oklahoma was ready for statehood in 1907, and five years later the sparsely settled territories of New Mexico and Arizona followed it into the Union, completing the political division of the nation.

Although the director of the census had spoken prematurely in 1890 when he declared that "the unsettled area has been so broken into by isolated bodies of settlement that there can hardly be said to be a frontier line," these events in the Southwest signaled the closing of an era of American history. Good lands scattered throughout the trans-Mississippi country still waited the settler's plow; actually four times as many acres were homesteaded after 1890 as before. But the day was drawing to an end when relatively cheap farms beckoned the dispossessed and the ambitious with the promise of a chance to begin life anew amidst nature's bounties. With the closing of the frontier the United States was on the threshold of a new era, where its people must face the problems of an expansionless existence for the first time in their history.

— 8 —

THE FRONTIER'S IMPACT ON AMERICAN LIFE

The passing of the frontier did not end its influence on the American people and their institutions. Three centuries of pioneering had endowed them with certain traits and characteristics that were too firmly implanted to be rapidly discarded; these remain today as the principal distinguishing features of the unique civilization of the United States. For the frontier was more than a westward-moving area promising individuals a greater degree of economic and social upward-mobility than they could find elsewhere; frontiering was a process through which artifacts, customs, and institutions imported from the Old World were adapted to suit conditions in the New. It was, in the words of Frederick Jackson Turner who first expounded the "frontier hypothesis," the area of most rapid "Americanization."

This was accomplished by the continuous re-evolution of society as men moved into the wilderness. They started westward with the "cultural baggage" acquired through generations of residence in compact communities: rigid governmental controls, diversified economic systems, a complex social structure, and a taste for the arts based on a rich cultural heritage. Some parts of this inheritance were discarded on the way west, for the hardships of migration made certain frills of civilization appear as expendable as the furniture, fancy clothes, and other non-essentials that were strewn along the overland trails by each passing caravan. More were abandoned in the primitive communities that took shape along the frontier, for in those isolated outposts, where ties with the past were few, where neighbors were widely scattered, and where the practical necessity of subduing stubborn nature seemed alone important, the customs and institutions that had proven useful in the compact societies of the East often appeared to be unworkable or outmoded. Amidst the lonely atmosphere of the forest or plains men readjusted their values and habits to the needs of the moment, and in doing so discarded a portion of their civilizing heritage.

This reversion toward the primitive was noticable in every phase of their social behavior. Simple associations of settlers were substituted for complex governmental systems. Each man undertook the task of supplying his family's economic needs as was necessary in a land where the nearest shoemaker or tailor or grocer was a week's journey away. Class distinctions underwent the revolution natural in a community where the skilled axman or the good rifle shot contributed more to society than a person of aristocratic lineage or inherited prestige. The complexities of life amidst a rigidly stratified social structure were forsaken as men and women sought pleasure in corn husking bees, barn dances, and cabin raisings. Cultural pursuits were ignored in an atmosphere where the multitudinous tasks essential to survival bred a new interest in material welfare and a lessening concern with esthetic pleasures. Men on the frontier moved far backward on the scale of civilization, although they clung tenaciously to portions of their heritage against the day when their children would lead a richer life than their own.

The regression usual in primitive communities was halted and eventually reversed as newcomers poured in to extend the clearings and alter the man-land ratio. Slowly the institutions necessary in a compact social order re-emerged: governmental controls were tightened with the creation of legislative, executive, and judicial bodies; economic specialization began as the interchange of goods increased; class distinctions were sharpened with the emergence of a new aristocracy; social activities grew more complex; cultural interests multiplied. Eventually a full-blown society emerged, but one that differed from those in Europe or the East on which it was based. The cultural baggage lost during migration, the impact of the unique environment, the acculturation that occurred as men of differing racial and geographical backgrounds met and mingled, and the variations inevitable in separate evolutions all contributed to the uniqueness of the resulting social order. As this new West merged with the East the pioneers placed their stamp on the civilization of the nation as a whole. The distinctive characteristics that distinguish the American people from those of Europe were partly the result of this recurring pioneering experience.

For the typical American, as Hector St. John de Creveoceur remarked in the eighteenth century, was indeed a "new man." He was materialistic in his interests, scornful of esthetic pursuits, and suspicious of "intellectuals," just as had been his pioneering forbears. He was more adaptable than the European, always ready to try new tools or techniques, and with little respect for tradition; frontiersmen developed these traits as they daily faced problems for which experience offered no solution. He was unusually mobile both physically and socially; a given place bound him no more firmly than it had his pioneering ancestors while like them he thought in terms of upward mobility where his job or social position were concerned. He was a congenital waster, building his whole economy on the concept of replacement rather than conservation, for he had failed as had the frontiersmen to learn that nature's bounties were exhaustible. Materialism, inventiveness, mobility, and exploitiveness remain characteristics of the American people today, even though they live in a nonexpanding world.

Equally traceable to the pioneering experience are the optimism and individualism so apparent in the United States. Certainly the usual frontiersman was an incurable optimist; he braved the wilderness only because of a compelling desire for improvement and firmly believed that continued progress would be his lot. Only this faith allowed backwoodsmen to endure the dangers and backbreaking toil of life in the West; their focus was on the future rather than the past. Nor did they want any interference from government or society as they tapped nature's riches in their unending quest for wealth. Confident that fortune would soon smile, they wanted only to be let alone. Even today Americans are known for their "rugged individualism" and their suspicion of "welfare state" concepts that have gained such headway in nonfrontier countries.

If pioneering converted men into optimists and individualists it also quickened their natural nationalistic impulses. The frontiersman was a nationalist of necessity. Only the central government could provide for his many needs: protection from the Indians, a favorable land policy, transportation outlets for his produce, protective tariffs to develop home markets. Impatient to achieve these ends, he was scornful of long-term planning and disdainful of constitutional limitations which interfered with his objectives. Frontier pressure during the nineteenth century prodded the nation into accepting the principle of loose construction and partially accounted for the enlarged activity of the federal government at the expense of the states. The United States today is still notable for its exaggerated nationalism, even though the realities of twentieth-century existence are enshrining internationalism as essential to survival in a shrinking world.

American faith in democracy, like that in nationalism, is partially traceable to the frontier heritage. That either democratic theory or practice originated in the backwoods is demonstrably untrue; both were well advanced when the conquest of the West began and both continued to receive stimulation from Europe during the eighteenth and nineteenth centuries. Yet frontier conditions tended to modify imported institutions along more democratic lines. In primitive communities the wide diffusion of land ownership created a natural demand that those with a stake in society should have a voice in society, while the common level of social and economic status and the absence of any prior leadership structure encouraged universal participation in government. With self-rule a brutal necessity due to the nonexistence of external controls, and with men and women accustomed to widespread participation in group affairs through cabin raisings, corn husking bees, and the like, it was natural that they should think in terms of political equality. Democratic practices came naturally to frontier groups, and with them an unswerving faith in democracy as a panacea for all the ills of the nation or the world.

That the distinctive traits of today's Americans are traceable solely to their pioneering heritage is as unthinkable as the belief that those characteristics have remained unaltered by industrialization and urbanization. On the other hand, denial that the frontier experience has exerted a continuing influence down to the present is impossible. The American people do display a versatility, a practical ingenuity, an earthy materialism, to a degree uncommon among Europeans. They do squander natural resources with an abandon shocking to others; they are a mobile people both physically and socially. In few other lands is nationalism carried to such extremes of isolationism or international arrogance, or the democratic ideal worshipped with such enthusiasm. Rarely do older societies display such indifference to esthetic creativity or such disrespect for intellectualism; seldom do they cling so tenaciously to the shibboleth of rugged individualism. Nor do Europeans enjoy to the same degree the rosy faith in the future, the heady optimism, the belief in the inevitability of progress, that are part of the national dream. These are pioneer traits, and they have been too firmly implanted to be entirely dislodged by the impact of twentieth-century industrialization.

Because of their persistence, the United States has found readjustment difficult to the modern closed-space existence in which escape to a frontier is impossible and the national economy no longer revitalized by the eastward flow of hitherto untapped natural resources. Nor can the transition be eased by the opening of new "frontiers"—of electricity, nuclear energy, even outer space— for none of these offers the opportunity for individual self-improvement that was provided by the cheap lands of the early West. The gradual awakening of Americans to their fate has led to an agonizing reappraisal of government's role in the economic life of the people and of the part to be played by the nation in the world community. This adjustment to the realities of the twentieth century has relegated some of the traits that proved so valuable in the conquest of the continent—arrogant nationalism, rugged individualism, unthinking wastefulness —to positions of lessening importance in popular thought. Yet other pioneer characteristics—faith in democracy and confidence in continued progress—equip the America of today to lead the world along the path toward the peace and security that have ever been the goals of mankind.

Part II

DOCUMENTS

— Document No. 1 —

GABRIEL ARTHUR'S ACCOUNT OF HIS EXPLORATIONS AND CAPTIVITY, 1673[1]

The first Anglo-American frontiersmen to interest themselves in the western lands that lay beyond the coastal plain were the fur traders whose posts fringed the Virginia backcountry. In the spring of 1673 one of these border barons, Captain Abraham Wood, sent James Needham, a freeman accustomed to wilderness life, and Gabriel Arthur, an illiterate indentured servant, to explore the southern Piedmont in quest of new trading opportunities. Three weeks of travel brought the two adventurers to the French Broad River of eastern Tennessee, where Needham was killed by Cherokee Indians who took Arthur into captivity. For the next year the young Englishman lived with the Cherokee, accompanying their war parties into West Florida and the Carolinas, before they consented to escort him back to Wood's post, Fort Henry. On this journey Arthur was taken from his captors by a Shawnee band whose village they raided, and narrowly escaped death when he and his guardians were set upon by a group of Occaneechi Indians. Safely in the fort at last, he described his adventures to Captain Wood, who repeated the story in a letter to a friend in London, written on August 22, 1674.

[1] Reprinted by permission of the publishers, The Arthur H. Clark Company, from *The First Explorations of the Trans-Allegheny Region by the Virginians, 1650-1764*, by Clarence W. Alvord and Lee Bidwood (Cleveland, 1912), pp. 221-225.

Now ye king must goe to give ye monetons a visit which were his friends, mony signifying water and ton great in theire language Gabriell must goe along with him They gett forth with sixty men and travelled tenn days due north and then arrived at ye monyton towne sittuated upon a very great river att which place ye tide ebbs and flowes. Gabriell swom in ye river severall times, being fresh water, this is a great towne and a great number of Indians belong unto it, and in ye same river Mr. Batt and Fallam were upon the head of it as you read in one of my first jornalls. This river runes north west out of ye westerly side of it goeth another very great river about a days journey lower where the inhabitance are an inumarable company of Indians, as the monytons told my man which is twenty dayes journey from one end to ye other of ye inhabitance, and all these are at warr with the Tomahitans. when they had taken theire leave of ye monytons they marched three days out of thire way to give a clap to some of that great nation, where they fell on with great courage and were as curagiously repullsed by theire enimise.

And heare Gabriell received shott with two arrows one of them in his thigh, which stopt his runing and soe was taken prisoner, for Indian vallour consists most in theire heeles for he that can run best is accounted ye best man. These Indians thought this Gabrill to be noe Tomahittan by ye length of his haire, for ye Tomahittans keepe theire haire close cut to ye end an enime may not take an advantage to lay hold of them by it. They tooke Gabriell and scowered his skin with water and ashes, and when they perceived his skin to be white they made very much of him and admire att his knife gunn and hatchett they tooke with him. They gave those thing to him a gaine. He made signes to them the gun was ye Tomahittons which he had a disire to take with him, but ye knife and hatchet he gave to ye king. they not knowing ye use of gunns, the king received it with great shewes of thankfulness for they had not any manner of iron instrument that hee saw amongst them whilst he was there they brought in a fatt beavor which they had newly

killd and went to swrynge [*sic*] it. Gabriell made signes
to them that those skins were good a mongst the white
people toward the sun riseing they would know by signes
how many such skins they would take for such a knife.
He told them foure and eight for such a hattchett and
made signes that if they would lett him return, he would
bring many things amongst them. they seemed to rejoyce
att it and carried him to a path that carried to ye Tomahittans gave him Rokahamony for his journey and soe
they departed, to be short. when he came to ye Tomahittans ye king had one short voyage more before hee could
bring in Gabriell and that was downe ye river, they live
upon in perriougers to kill hoggs, beares and sturgion
which they did incontinent by five dayes and nights. They
went down ye river and came to ye mouth of ye salts
where they could not see land but the water not above
three foot deepe hard sand. By this meanes wee know
this is not ye river ye Spanyards live upon as Mr. Needham did thinke. Here they killd many swine, sturgin and
beavers and barbicued them, soe returned and were fifteen
dayes runing up a gainst ye streame but noe mountainous
land to bee seene but all levell.

After they had made an end of costing of it about ye
10th day of May 1674, ye king with eighteen more of
his people laden with goods begin theire journey to come
to Forte Henry at ye falls of Appomattock river in
Charles City County in Virginia, they were not disturbed
in all theire travels untill they came to Sarah, w[h]ere ye
Occhenechees weare as I tould you before to waite Gabrills coming. There were but foure Occohenechees Indians there soe that they durst not adventure to attempt
any violent action by day. Heare they say they saw the
small truck lying under foot that Indian John had scattered and thrown about when he had killd Mr. Needham.
when it grew prity late in ye night ye Occhenee began
to worke thire plot and made an alaram by an hubbub
crying out the towne was besett with in numarable company of strange Indians this puts the towne people into
a sodane fright many being betweene sleepeing and wake-
ing, away rune ye Tomahittans and leave all behind them,
and a mongst ye rest was Gabrills two pieces of gold and
chaine in an Indian bagge away slipe Gabriell and ye

Spanish Indian boy which he brought with him and hide themselves in ye bushes.

After ye Tomahittans were gon ye foure Occhenechees for there came no more to disturb them, made diligent search for Gabriell. Ye moone shining bright Gabriell saw them, but he lying under covert of ye bushes could not be seene by that Indians. In ye morning ye Occhenechees haveing mist of thire acme passed home and Gabriell came into ye town againe and four of ye Tomahittans packs hires foure Sarrah Indians to carry them to Aeno. Here he mett with my man I had sent out soe long ago before to inquire for news despratly sick of ye flux, here hee could not gett any to goe forth with his packs for feare of ye Occhenechees, soe he left them and adventured himselfe with ye Spanish Indian boy. ye next day came before night in ye sight of ye Occhenechees towne undiscovered and there hid himselfe untill it was darke and then waded over into ye iland where ye Occhenechees are seated, strongly fortified by nature and that makes them soe insolent for they are but a handfull of people, besides what vagabonds repaire to them it beeing a receptackle for rogues. Gabriell escapes cleaurely through them and soe wades out on this side and runs for it all night. Theirie food was huckleburyes, which ye woods were full of att that time and on ye 18th June with ye boy arrived att my house, praise be to God for it.

— Document No. 2 —

FRONTIER LIFE IN THE COLONIAL BACKCOUNTRY[2]

As small farmers followed the fur traders into the hilly uplands beyond the fall-line they felt the full impact of America's wilderness environment for the first time. Their adjustment to this strange new world transformed them into typical frontiersmen, skilled in the use of the ax and rifle, and far more at home in the trackless forest than in the streets of Philadelphia or Williamsburg. Their transmutation was nowhere better dramatized than in the clothes that they wore and the homes in which they lived. These were described by a traveler in the Virginia-Pennsylvania backcountry, Joseph Doddridge, as they appeared about the middle of the eighteenth century.

𝄌   𝄌   𝄌

On the frontiers, and particularly amongst those who were much in the habit of hunting, and going on scouts, and campaigns, the dress of the men was partly Indian, and partly that of civilized nations.

The hunting shirt was universally worn. This was a kind of loose frock, reaching half way down the thighs, with large sleeves, open before, and so wide as to lap over a foot or more when belted. The cape was large, and sometimes handsomely fringed with a ravelled piece of cloth of a different colour from that of the hunting shirt itself. The bosom of this dress served as a wallet to hold a chunk of bread, cakes, jirk, tow for wiping the barrel of the rifle, or any other necessary for the hunter or warrior. The belt which was always tied behind answered

---

[2] Joseph Doddridge, *Notes on the Settlement and Indian Wars, of the Western Parts of Virginia and Pennsylvania* (Wellsburgh, Virginia, 1824), pp. 113-115 and pp. 134-137.

several purposes, besides that of holding the dress together. In cold weather the mittens, and sometimes the bullet-bag occupied the front part of it. To the right side was suspended the tomahawk and to the left the scalping knife in its leathern sheath. The hunting shirt was generally made of linsey, sometimes of coarse linen, and a few of dressed deer skins. These last were very cold and uncomfortable in wet weather. The shirt and jacket were of the common fashion. A pair of drawers or breeches and leggings, were the dress of the thighs, and legs, a pair of mocassons answered for the feet much better than shoes. These were made of dressed deer skin. They were mostly made of a single piece with a gathering seam along the top of the foot, and another from the bottom of the heel, without gathers as high as the ankle joint or a little higher. Flaps were left on each side to reach some distance up the legs. These were nicely adapted to the ankles, and lower part of the leg by thongs of deer skin, so that no dust, gravel, or snow could get within the mocasson.

The mocassons in ordinary use cost but a few hours labour to make them. This was done by an instrument denominated a mocasson awl, which was made of the backspring of an old claspknife. This awl with its buckshorn handle was an appendage of every shot pouch strap, together with a roll of buckskin for mending the mocassons. This was the labour of almost every evening. They were sewed together and patched with deer skin thongs, or whangs as they were commonly called.

In cold weather the mocassons were well stuffed with deers hair, or dry leaves, so as to keep the feet comfortably warm; but in wet weather it was usually said that wearing them was 'A decent way of going barefooted;' and such was the fact, owing to the spongy texture of the leather of which they were made.

Owing to the defective covering of the feet, more than to any other circumstance the greater number of our hunters and warriors were afflicted with the rheumatism in their limbs. Of this disease they were all apprehensive in cold or wet weather, and therefore always slept with their feet to the fire to prevent or cure it as well as they could. This practice unquestionably had a very salutary effect, and prevented many of them from becoming confirmed cripples in early life. . . .

I will proceed to state the usual manner of settling a young couple in the world.

A spot was selected on a piece of land of one of the parents, for their habitation. A day was appointed shortly after their marriage for commencing the work of building their cabin. The fatigue party consisted of choppers, whose business it was to fell the trees and cut them off at proper lengths. A man with a team for hauling them to the place, and arranging them, properly assorted, at the sides and ends of the building, a carpenter, if such he might be called, whose business it was to search the woods for a proper tree for making clapboards for the roof. The tree for the purpose must be straight grained and from three to four feet in diameter. The boards were split four feet long, with a large frow, and as wide as the timber would allow. They were used without plaining or shaving. Another division were employed in getting puncheons for the floor of the cabin; this was done by splitting trees, about eighteen inches in diameter, and hewing the faces of them with a broad axe. They were half the length of the floor they were intended to make.

The materials for the cabin were mostly prepared on the first day and sometimes the foundation laid in the evening. The second day was allotted for the raising.

In the morning of the next day the neighbours collected for the raising. The first thing to be done was the election of four corner men, whose business it was to notch and place the logs. The rest of the company furnished them with the timbers. In the meantime the boards and puncheons were collecting for the floor and roof, so that by the time the cabin was a few rounds high the sleepers and floor began to be laid. The door was made by sawing or cutting the logs in one side so as to make an opening about three feet wide. This opening was secured by upright pieces of timber about three inches thick through which holes were bored into the ends of the logs for the purpose of pinning them fast. A similar opening, but wider, was made at the end for the chimney. This was built of logs and made large to admit of a back and jams of stone. At the square, two end logs projected a foot or eighteen inches beyond the wall to receive the butting poles, as they were called, against which the ends of the first row of clap boards was supported. The roof was formed by making the end logs shorter until a single log formed the comb of the roof, on these logs the clap boards were placed, the ranges of them laping some distance over those next below them and kept in their places by logs, placed at proper distances upon them.

The roof, and sometimes, the floor were finished on the same day of the raising. A third day was commonly spent by a few carpenters in leveling off the floor, making a clap board door and a table. This last was made of a split slab and supported by four round legs set in auger holes. Some three-legged stools were made in the same manner. Some pins stuck in the logs at the back of the house supported some clap boards which served for shelves for the table furniture. A single fork, placed with its lower end in a hole in the floor and the upper end fastened to a joist served for a bed stead, by placing a pole in the fork with one end through a crack between the logs of the wall. This front pole was crossed by a shorter one within the fork, with its outer end through another crack. From the front pole, through a crack between the logs of the end of the house, the boards were put on which formed the bottom of the bed. Some times other poles, were pinned to the fork a little distance above these, for the purpose of supporting the front and foot of the bed, while the walls were the supports of its back and head. A few pegs around the wall for a display of the coats of the women, and the hunting shirts of the men, and two small forks or bucks horns to a joist for the rifle and shot pouch, completed the carpenter work.

In the meantime masons were at work. With the heart pieces of the timber of which the clapboards were made, they made billets for chunking up the cracks between the logs of the cabin and chimney, a large bed of mortar was made for daubing up those cracks; a few stones formed the back and jambs of the chimney.

The cabin being finished, the ceremony of house warming took place, before the young couple were permitted to move into it.

The house warming was a dance of a whole night's

continuance, made up of the relations of the bride and groom, and their neighbours. On the day following the young couple took possession of their new mansion.

— Document No. 3 —

THE ATTACK ON FORT PRESQ'ISLE IN PONTIAC'S REBELLION, 1763[3]

Each advance of the farming frontier was at the expense of the Indians, who were periodically driven to warfare in a vain effort to retain their hunting grounds. One of the most devastating of these wars was Pontiac's Rebellion, which began in May, 1763, when Chief Pontiac, an Ottawa warrior, led his tribesmen in an attack on the British fort at Detroit. This assault was repulsed, but as news of the Detroit uprising goaded Indians all over the West into war, other forts were less fortunate. One that fell before the onslaught was Fort Presq'isle in northwestern Pennsylvania. A vivid description of the attack was written by Edward Smyth, a commissary stationed at the fort, in a letter to Colonel Henry Bouquet, his commanding officer.

✓   ✓   ✓

On the 21st June at break of Day, We first saw the Savages, Who crossed the Run near where the Batteaux lay, and crept under the Banks of the Lake and Sawpits, being covered from Us, they continued without attempt-

[3] Sylvester K. Stevens and Donald H. Kent, eds., *Wilderness Chronicles of Northwestern Pennsylvania* (Harrisburg, 1941), pp. 253-254. Reprinted by permission of the Pennsylvania Historical and Museum Commission.

ing any Thing till Sun Rise; when they appeared and Hooped in their usual Manner. The Commanding Officer having ordered the Men not to fire until the Savages began by which Means they (being very near) on receiving our first Fire Sprung into the Ditch, where they continued, firing at intervals, throwing Fire Balls, Dirt, and Stones at Us but to no Purpose, They also Sheltered themselves behind the Bake house, and Houses within the Breast Work, where finding they could not hurt us, they began under a Cover of Plank, which they got from the Necessary House to sap the Bank, which they Effected with long Poles as they told me, so that they fired at Us pretty smartly in the Night, without our being able to See the flash of their Guns.

The same Day our Water failing, the Soldiers cut out a Subterranean Passage to the Well, which in case of Fire would Plentifully supply us with Water, as well as for our Drink, the Well having been cleaned some little Time before. At this the Men worked chearfully and performed every other Duty with great Spirit.

The next morning being the 22d the Savages fired very little, and not till late in the Morning; being convinced they could not hurt us, and their Powder (I believe) scarce, They lay by till afternoon, in which Interval they prepared their Arrows for firing the Roof. They began by firing the Command[in]g Officers House. The Wind being pretty brisk it blew on the Bastion of the Block House but did no Damage, They then set the Roof of the Block House on fire in two places, at the same time firing briskly on Us, to prevent our putting it out: But by beating off some Shingles, We in about a Quarter of an Hour extinguished it: They likewise attempted to fire the Loggs of the House, but the Arrows burning only a Small hole dropt out without Effect.

The fire being out, and the Savages attempting nothing further, The Commanding Officer called the Men together to know their Opinions. They declared, (excepting two Men) They were willing to defend the House. My opinion being asked, I told them: having only a Single Life to lose, I would be governed by their resolutions, but thought it possible to defend the House longer, as I was persuaded We could always extinguish the Fire, and had nothing else to fear, and at the same Time put them in Mind of their Treacherous design upon Detroit, how they broke the Capitulation at Fort William Henry and Fort Loudoun, and that We could not expect any other usage.

The Commanding Officer considering that We had but about a Month's Provision, that all communication was cut off, no Possibility of receiving any relief from Fort Pitt, or Niagara, and that the longer we resisted, we should make them the more desperate, declared his opinion of Speaking to them, and to know what they wanted, this was Effected by means of a Frenchman, and an English Man among the Indians: and as they promised very fair to escort us to the first Garrison; it ended with a Surrender of the Place, and everything in it next Morning, being the 23d of June 1763."

— Document No. 4 —

THE FRONTIER ADVANCE INTO KENTUCKY[4]

With the decisive defeat of the western Indians in Pontiac's Rebellion, adventurous frontiersmen began pushing through the gaps in the Appalachian Mountains to begin the conquest of western Pennsylvania, eastern Tennessee, and Kentucky. The principal promoter of Kentucky's blue-grass country was Judge Richard Henderson, a wealthy North Carolina planter and land speculator, whose Transylvania Company illegally purchased the region from the Cherokee Indians at the Treaty of Sycamore

[4] Thomas Speed, *The Wilderness Road* (Louisville, 1886), pp. 36-38.

Shoals in March, 1775. Even before the treaty was signed, Henderson sent a party of axmen under Daniel Boone to cut the Wilderness Road from Cumberland Gap to his new domain. A few days later he started westward himself, accompanied by a party of would-be settlers. One of these, William Calk of Virginia, recorded the story of their journey in a diary notable for its startlingly original spelling.

fryday 7th-this morning is a very bad snowey morning we still continue at Camp being in number about 40 men and some neagros this Eaven Comes a letter from Capt. Boone at caintuck of the indians doing mischief and some turns back.

Saturday 8th-We all pack up and started crost Cumberland gap about one o'clock this Day Met a good maney peopel turned Back for fear of the indians but our Company goes on Still with good courage we come to a very ugly Creek with steep Banks and have it to cross several times on this Creek we camp this night.

Sunday 9th-this morning we wait at camp for the cattel to Be drove up to kill a Beef tis late before they come and peopel makes out a little snack and agree to go on till Night we git to cumberland River and there we camp meet 2 more men turn Back.

Monday 10th-this is a lowry morning and very like for Rain and we keep at Camp this day and some goes out a hunting and I and two more goes up a very large mountain near the tops we saw the track of two indians and whear they had lain under some Rocks some of the company went over the River a bufelo hunting but found none at night Capt. hart comes up with his packs and there they hide some of thier lead to lighten thier packs that they may travel faster.

tuesday 11th-this a very loury morning and like for Rain but we all agree to start Early and we cross Cumberland River and travell Down it about 10 miles through some turrabel cainbrakes as we went down abrams mair Ran into the River with her load and swam over he followed her and got on her and made her swim back agin it is a very raney Eavening we take up Camp near Richard

Creek they kill a beef Mr. Drake Bakes Bread without washing his hands we Keep Sentry this Night for fear of the Indians.

Wednesday 12th-this is a Raney morning But we pack up and go on we come to Richland Creek it is high we tote our packs over on a tree and swim our horses over and there we meet another Companey going Back they tell such News Abram and Rake is afraid to go aney farther there we camp this night.

thursday 13th-this morning the weather seems to brake and Be fair Abram and Drake turn Back we go on and git to loral River we come to a creek Before wheare we are able to unload and to take our packs over on a log this day we meet about 20 more turning Back we are obliged to toat our packs over loral river and swim our horses one hors ran in with his pack and lost it in the river and they got it agin.

Fryday 14th-this is a clear morning with a smart frost we go on and have a very miry Road and camp this night on a creek of loral river and are surprised at camp by a wolf.

Satterday 15th-clear with a Small frost we start early we meet some men that turns and goes With us we travel this Day through the plais caled the Bressh and cross Rochcass river and camp ther this Night and have fine food for our horses.

sunday 16th-cloudy and warm we start early and go on about 2 miles down the river and then turn up a creek that we crost about 50 times some very bad foards with a great Deal of very good land on it in the Eavening we git over to the waters of Caintuck and go a little down the creek and there we camp keep sentel the fore part of the night it Rains very har all night.

monday 17th-this is a very rany morning But breaks about a 11 oclock and we go on and camp this Night in several companeys on some of the creeks of Caintuck.

tuesday 18th-fair and cool and we go on about 10 oclock we meet 4 men from Boons camp that caim to cunduck us on we camp this night just on the Beginning of the good land near the Blue lock they kill 2 bofelos this Eavening.

wednesday 19th-smart frost this morning they kill 3

bofelos about 11 oclock we come to where the indians fired on Boons company and killed 2 men and a dog and wounded one man in the thigh we campt this night on otter creek.

thursday 20th-this morning is clear and cool. We start early and git Down to caintuck to Boons foart about 12 o'clock where we stop they come out to meet us and welcome us in with a voley of guns.

fryday 21st-warm this Day they begin laying off lots in the town and preparing for people to go to work to make corn.

Satterday 22nd-they finish laying out lots this Eavening I went a-fishing and caught 3 cats they meet in the night to draw for chose of lots but perfer it till morning.

Sunday, 23rd-this morning the peopel meets and draws for chois of lots this is a very warm day.

monday 24th-We all view our lots and some Dont like them about 12 oclock the combses come to town and Next morning they make them a bark canew and set off down the river to meet their Companey.

tuesday 25th-in the eavening we git us a plaise at the mouth of the creek and begin clearing.

Wednesday 26th-We Begin Building us a house and a plaise of Defense to Keep the Indians off this day we being to live without bread.

thursday 27th-Raney all Day But We Still keep about our house.

Satterday 29th-We git our house kivered with Bark and move our things into it at Night and Begin housekeeping Eanock Smith Robert Whitledge and myself.

— Document No. 5 —

GEORGE ROGERS CLARK'S CAMPAIGN AGAINST VINCENNES, 1779[5]

The pioneers who reared their cabins in the over-mountain country suffered greatly when the outbreak of the American Revolution plunged the West into a new era of Indian warfare. Goaded on by their British allies, the red men carried on their attacks with such devastating success that by 1778 only three Kentucky "stations" were still occupied, and these were under almost constant siege. Realizing that the raids could be stopped only by carrying the war against the enemy, a young Kentuckian named George Rogers Clark secured a commission from Virginia, raised a small army of frontiersmen, and captured the settlements at Kaskaskia and Cahokia in the Illinois country as a prelude to a march on the principal British post at Detroit. The commander of that fort, rather than waiting to be attacked, moved forward to Vincennes. When news of this maneuver reached Clark at Kaskaskia in February, 1779, he started for Vincennes at once with 172 men. His own account of that march reveals the unbelievable suffering endured by the frontiersmen before the British post was reached and captured.

✓ ✓ ✓

On the 20th the water guard decoyed on shore a Boat with 5 Frenchmen and some provitions on board they on their way to Join a party of Hunters down the River

---

[5] James A. James, ed., *The George Rogers Clark Papers, 1771-1781, Collections of the Illinois State Historical Library, VIII*. (Springfield, Illinois, 1912), pp. 273-277. Reprinted by permission of the Trustees of the Illinois State Historical Library.

they informed us that we not discovered that the Inhabitants ware well disposed towards us that they had greatly strenghened the fort, which was quite finished that their numbers was nearly the same as when Mr Vigo left the place in short they gave us every Information we wished for and of two Vessels that they said was a drift up the River Cap^{tn} Worthington Recovered one having now two small Vessels Early of the 21st the Crossing of our Troops comenced and was landed and Landed on a small rising called the Mamel leaving our Baggage Cap^{tn} J. Williams serching for a passage gave chase to a canoe but could not bring to the men that we had taken said that it was Impossible that we could make the Town that Night or at all with our Vessels but recollecting what we had done we thought otherways—pushed into the water and Marched a League to what is call the upper Mamell being frequently to the arm pits in water hear we Incampted our men yet in spirits from the hopes of their Fatiegue soon being at an end and their wishes acomplish in geting in in contact with the Enemy this last march through the water was so far Superiour to any thing the French Men had an Idea of that they were backward in speaking said that the nearest Land to us was a small League call the Shugar Camps on the bank of the River a canoe was dispatch of and Returned without finding that we could pass I went in her myself and sounded the water found as deep as to my neck I Returned with a design to have the men Transported on board the canoes to the Shugar Camp which I new would spend the whole Day and Insuing night as the Vessels would pass but slowly through the Bushes the loss of so much time to men half starved was a matter of consequence I would have given now a good deal for a Days provition or for one of our Horses I returned but slowly to the Troops giving my self time to think on our arrival all ran to hear what was the Report every Eye was fixed on me I unfortunately Spoke Serious to one of the Officers—the whole was allarmed without knowing what I said the ran from one to another bewailing their Situation I Viewed their confution for about one minute. Whispered to those near me to [do] as I did—ameditely took some water in my hand poured on Powder Blacked my face gave the war hoop and marched into the water without saying a word the party gased and fell in one after another without saying a word like a flock of sheep. I ordered those that was near me to begin a favourite song of theirs it soon passed through the Line and the whole went on chearfully I now Intended have them Transported across the deepest part of the water but when geting about waist deep one of the men Informed me that he thought he felt a path we examined and found it so and concluded that it keep on the Highest ground which it did and by pains to follow it we got to the Shugar camp without the least difficulty and what gave the allarm at the former proved fortunate whare their was about half an Acre of dry ground at least not under water whare we took up our Lodgings The French men that we had taken on the River appeared to be uneasy at our situation They beged that they might be permitted to go in the two canoes to Town in they night that they would bring from their own Houses provitions without a possibility of any perons knowing it that some of our men should go with them as a surety of their good conduct that it was impossible we could march from that place untill the water fell that would be in a few days for the plain befor for upwards of three miles was covered too deep to march some of the Selicited that it might be done I would not suffer it by no means I never could well account for this piece [of] obstinacy and give satisfactory reasons to myself or any body else why I denied a proposition apparently so easy to Execute and so much advantage but some thing seemed to Tell me that it should not be done and it was not. The most of the weather that we had on this march was moist and warm for the season this was the coldest Night we had the Ice in the morning was from 1/2 to 3/4 Inch thick near the shoars and in still water the Morning was the finest we had had on our march. A little after sun-Rise I Lectured the whole what I said to them I forget but it may be easily Imagined by a person that could possess my affections for them at that time Concluded by informing them that surmounting the plain that was then in full View and Reaching the opposite woods would put an End to their fatiegue that in a few Hours they would have a sight of their long wish for Object and amediately stept into the water without waiting

for any Reply a Huza took place as we Gen^ly March
through the water in a line as it was much Easiest before
a third Entered I Halted and further to prove the Men
and having some suspition of three or four Hollowed to
Maj^r Bowman order him to fall in the rear with 25 men
and put to death any man that refused to March that we
wished to have no such person among us the whole gave
a cry of apperbation that it was Right and on we went
This was the most Trying of all the difficulties we had
experienced I Gen^ly keep 15 or 20 of the strongest men
Next myself and Judging from my own feeling what must
be that of of other geting about the Middle of the plain
the water about need deep I found myself sensibly failing
as their was hear no Trees or Bushes for the men to support them selves by I doubted that many of the most weak
would be drownd I order the canoes to make the Land
discharge their Loading and ply backwards and forwards
with all diligence and pick up the men and to Incourage
the party sent some of the strongest men forward with
orders when they got to a certain distance to pass the
word back that the water was geting [shallower] and
when geting near the woods to cry out Land This strata-
gem had its desired effect the men Incouraged by exerted
themselves almost beyond their abilities the weak holding
by the stronger and frequently one with two others holt
this was of Infinite advantage to the weak but the water
never got shallower but continued deepening geting to
the woods whare they expected Land the Water was up to
my shoulders but gaining those woods was of great consequence all the Low men and Weakly Hung to the Trees
and floated on the old logs untill they ware taken of by
the Canoes the strong and Tall got ashore and built fires
many would reach the shore and fall with their bodies
half in the water not being able to Support themselves
with out it this was a delightfull Dry spot of Ground of
about Ten Acres we soon found that the fires answered
no purpose but that two strong men taking a weaker one
by the Arms was the only way to recover him and being
a delightfull Day it soon did. But unfortunately as if designed by Providence a Canoe of Indian squaws and Children was coming up to the Town and took through part of
this plain as a nigh way was discovered by our Canoes as

they ware out after the men they gave chase and took
them on Board of which was near half Quarter of Buffaloe
some corn Tallow Kettles &c this was a grand prise and
was Invaluable. Broath was amediately made and served
out to the most weak by [but] with great care most of the
whole got a little but a great many would not tast it but
gave their part to the weakly Jocosely saying something
cheary to their comrades. this little refreshment and fine
weather by the afternoon gave new life to the whole
crossing a narrow deep Lake in the Canoes and marching
some distance we came to a Copse of Timber called the
warriours Island we ware now in full View of the Fort
and Town not a srub betwen us at about two miles distance every man now feasted his Eyes and forgot that he
had suffered any thing that all that had pass^d was owing
to good policy and nothing but what a man could bear
and that a solider had no Right to think &c passing from
one extream to another which is common in such cases
it was now we had to Display our Abilities the plain betwen us and the Town was not a perfect level the sunken
ground was covered with water full of Ducks we observed
several men on Hors back out shooting of them within
half Mile of us and sent out as many of our active young
French men to decoy and take one of them prisoner in
such a manner as not to allarm the others which they did
the Information we got from this person was similar to
those we took on the River excep that of the British that
Eaevening having Compleated the wall of the Fort &c that
their was a good many Indians in Town our situation was
now Truly critical no possibility of Retreating in case of
Defeat in full View of a Town that at this time had upwards of Six Hundred Men in it Troops Inhabitants and
Indians. The Crew of the Gally though not fifty men
would have been now a Reinforcement of Imence Magni-
tude to our Little Army (if I may so call it) but we would
not think of them we ware now in the situation that I
had Laboured to get our selves in the Idea of being made
prisoner was foreign almost to Every man as the expected
nothing but Torture from the savages if they fell into
their Hands our Fate was now to be determined probably
in a few Hours we knew that nothing but the Most daring
conduct could Insure suckcess.

— Document No. 6 —

INDIAN WARFARE IN THE NORTHWEST: ST. CLAIR'S DEFEAT, 1791[6]

American victory in the Revolution did not end Indian warfare in the West, for the red men were left disgruntled by the defeat of their red-coated allies and were encouraged by over-enthusiastic British agents to believe that hostilities would begin again. In this mood they renewed their raids on the interior settlements in 1789 and 1790, as they talked boldly of driving the "Big Knives" from the country north of the Ohio. President George Washington attempted to meet this threat in 1790 by sending an army under the aging General Josiah Harmar against the Indians, but the inept commander proved no match for his foes and was soundly defeated. A year later a second expedition headed by General Arthur St. Clair started northward from the Ohio toward the Maumee River. Some fifty miles from their objective, they were surprised on November 4, 1791, by an Indian attack that cost the lives of 630 of St. Clair's three thousand men. One of the soldiers, Major Ebenezer Denny, described the defeat in his journal.

✓   ✓   ✓

The troops paraded this morning at the usual time, and had been dismissed from the lines but a few minutes, the sun not yet up, when the woods in front rung with the yells and fire of the savages. The poor militia, who were but three hundred yards in front, had scarcely time to

[6] "Military Journal of Major Ebenezer Denny," *Memoirs of the Historical Society of Pennsylvania,* VII (Philadelphia, 1860), pp. 369-372.

return a shot—they fled into our camp. The troops were under arms in an instant, and a smart fire from the front line met the enemy. It was but a few minutes, however, until the men were engaged in every quarter. The enemy from the front filed off to the right and left, and completely surrounded the camp, killed and cut off nearly all the guards, and approached close to the lines. They advanced from one tree, log, or stump or another, under cover of the smoke of our fire. The artillery and musketry made a tremendous noise, but did little execution. The Indians seemed to brave everything, and when fairly fixed around us they made no noise other than their fire, which they kept up very constant and which seldom failed to tell, although scarcely heard. Our left flank, probably from the nature of the ground, gave way first; the enemy got possession of that part of the encampment, but it being pretty clear ground, they were too much exposed and were soon repulsed. Was at this time with the General engaged toward the right; he was on foot and led the party himself that drove the enemy and regained our ground on the left. The battalions in the rear charged several times and forced the savages from their shelter, but they always turned with the battalions and fired upon them back; indeed they seemed not to fear anything we could do. They could skip out of reach of the Bayonet and return, as they pleased. They were visible only when raised by a charge. The ground was literally covered with the dead. The wounded were taken to the centre, where it was thought most safe, and where a great many who had quit their posts unhurt, had crowded together. The General, with other officers, endeavored to rally these men, and twice they were taken out to the lines. It appeared as if the officers had been singled out; a very great proportion fell, or were wounded and obliged to retire from the lines early in the action. General Butler was among the latter, as well as several other of the most experienced officers. The men being thus left with few officers, became fearful, despaired of success, gave up the fight, and to save themselves for the moment, abandoned entirely their duty and ground, and crowded in toward the centre of the field, and no exertions could put them in any order even for defense; perfectly ungovernable. The enemy at length got possession of the artillery, though not until the officers were all killed but one, and he badly wounded, and the men almost all cut off, and not until the pieces were spiked. As our lines were deserted the Indians contracted theirs until their shot centered from all point, and now meeting with little opposition, took more deliberate aim and did great execution. Exposed to a cross fire, men and officers were seen falling in every direction; the distress too of the wounded made the scene such as can scarcely be conceived; a few minutes longer, and a retreat would have been impossible. The only hope left was, that perhaps the savages would be so taken up with the camp as not to follow. Delay was death; no preparation could be made; numbers of brave men must be left a sacrifice, there was no alternative. It was past nine o'clock, when repeated orders were given to charge toward the road. The action had continued between two and three hours. Both officers and men seemed confounded, incapable of doing anything; they could not move until it was told that a retreat was intended. A few officers put themselves in front, the men followed, the enemy gave way, and perhaps not being aware of the design, we were for a few minutes left undisturbed. The stoutest and most active now took the lead, and those who were foremost in breaking the enemy's line, were soon left behind. At the moment of the retreat, one of the few horses saved had been procured for the General; he was on foot until then; I kept by him, and he delayed to see the rear. The enemy soon discovered the movement and pursued, though not more than four or five miles, and but few so far; they turned to share the spoil. Soon after the firing ceased, I was directed to endeavor to gain the front, and if possible, to cause a short halt that the rear might get up. I had been on horseback from the first alarm, and well mounted; pushed forward, but met with so many difficulties and interruptions from the people, that I was two hours at least laboring to reach the front. With the assistance of two or three officers I caused a short halt, but the men grew impatient and would move on. I got Lieutenants Sedam and Morgan, with half a dozen stout men, to fill up the road and to move slowly, I halted myself until the General came up. By this time the remains of the army had got somewhat compact, but in the most miserable and defenseless state. The wounded who came off left their arms in the field, and one-half of the others threw theirs away on the retreat. The road for miles was covered with firelocks, cartridge boxes and regimentals. How fortunate that the pursuit was discontinued; a single Indian might have followed with safety upon either flank. Such a panic had seized the men, that I believe it would not have been possible to have brought any of them to engage again.

— Document No. 7 —

FRONTIER TYPES ON THE OHIO VALLEY FRONTIER[7]

When a well-trained army under General Anthony Wayne in 1794 avenged St. Clair's defeat and soundly punished the Indians at the Battle of Fallen Timbers, the Ohio Valley was at last safe for settlers. They poured into the region in an ever-growing flood during the years that followed, until their settlements extended over most of Ohio and filled the southern portions of Indiana and Illinois when the Panic of 1819 temporarily slowed migration. There, beyond the Appalachians that cut off their intercourse with Europe or the East, these "Men of the Western Waters" developed characteristics that marked them as a race apart, despite all of their efforts to cling to the civilization that they had abandoned. An English

[7] Reprinted by permission of the publishers, The Arthur H. Clark Company, from *Personal Narrative of Travels in Virginia, Maryland, Pennsylvania, Ohio, Indiana, Kentucky; and of a Residence in the Illinois Territory: 1817-1818,* by Elias P. Fordham (Cleveland, 1906), pp. 125-129.

traveler, Elias P. Fordham, commented on the uniqueness of western culture as he observed it during a trip through the valley in 1818.

✓   ✓   ✓

The people who live on these frontiers may be divided into four classes,—not perfectly distinct yet easily distinguishable.

1st. The hunters, a daring, hardy, race of men, who live in miserable cabins, which they fortify in times of War with the Indians, whom they hate but much resemble in dress and manners. They are unpolished, but hospitable, kind to Strangers, honest and trustworthy. They raise a little Indian corn, pumpkins, hogs, and sometimes have a Cow or two, and two or three horses belonging to each family: But their rifle is their principal means of support. They are the best marksmen in the world, and such is their dexterity that they will shoot an apple off the head of a companion. Some few use the bow and arrow. I have spent 7 or 8 weeks with these men, have had opportunities of trying them, and believe they would sooner give me the last shirt off their backs, than rob me of a charge of powder. Their wars with the Indians have made them vindictive. This class cannot be called first Settlers, for they move every year or two.

2^d. class. First settlers;—a mixed set of hunters and farmers. They possess more property and comforts than the first class; yet they are a half barbarous race. They follow the range pretty much; selling out when the Country begins to be well settled, and their cattle cannot be entirely kept in the woods.

3^d. class.—is composed of enterprising men from Kentucky and the Atlantic States. This class consists of Young Doctors, Lawyers, Storekeepers, farmers, mechanics &c, who found towns, trade, speculate in land, and begin the fabric of Society. There is in this class every *gradation* of *intellectual* and *moral* character; but the general tone of Social manners is yet too much relaxed. There is too much reliance upon personal prowess, and the laws have not yet acquired sufficient energy to prevent violence.

Such are the Inhabitants of the Southern parts of Indiana, and of Shawanoe town, St. Louis, St. Genevieve, and the large settlements on the Mississippi.

4th. class—old settlers, rich, independent, farmers, wealthy merchants, possessing a good deal of information, a knowledge of the world, and an enterprising spirit. Such are the Ohio men, Western Pennsylvanians, Kentuckians and Tennessee men. The young men have a military taste, and most of them have served in the late war. They were great duellists, but now the laws against duelling are more strictly enforced; they carry dirks, and sometimes decide a dispute on the spot. Irritable and dissipated in youth, yet they are generally steady and active in Manhood. They undertake with facility, and carry on with unconquerable ardour, any business or speculation that promises great profit, and sustain the greatest losses with a firmness that resembles indifference.

You will perceive from this slight sketch, which I have made as impartially as I am able, that the Backwoods men, as they are called somewhat contemptuously by the Inhabitants of the Atlantic States, are admirably adapted by Nature and education for the scenes they live and act in. The prominent feature of their character is power. The young value themselves on their courage, the old on their shrewdness. The veriest villains have something grand about them. They expect no mercy and they shew no fear; "every man's hand is against them, and their hand is against every man's."

As social Comforts are less under the protection of the laws here, than in old countries, friendship and good neighbourhood are more valued. A man of good character is an acquisition; not that there is a small proportion of such men, but because the bad are as undisguisedly bad, as their opposites are professedly good. This is not the land of Hypocrisy. It would not here have its reward. Religion is not the road to worldly respectability, nor a possession of it the cloak to immortality.

I wish I could give you a correct idea of the perfect equality that exists among these republicans. A Judge leaves the Court house, shakes hands with his fellow citizens and retires to his loghouse. The next day you will find him holding his own plough. The Lawyer has the title of Captain, and serves in his Military capacity under his neighbour, who is a farmer and a Colonel. The shop keeper sells a yard of tape, and sends shiploads of produce to Orleans; he travels 2000 miles a year; he is a good hunter, and has been a soldier; he dresses and talks as well as a London Merchant, and probably has a more extensive range of ideas; at least he has fewer prejudices. One prejudice, however, nothing will induce him to give up—he thinks the Americans in general, and particularly those of his own state, are the best soldiers in the world. Such is the native Shopkeeper: the Eastern Emigrant is very different.

I have not seen an effeminate, or a feeble man, in mind or body, belonging to these Western Countries. The most ignorant, compared with men of the same standing in England, are well informed. Their manners are coarse; but they have amongst themselves a code of politeness, which they generally observe. Drinking whisky is the greatest pest, the most fertile source of disorders, amongst them. When intoxicated by it, they sometimes fight most furiously. In this they resemble the Lower Irish.

There is an universal spirit of enquiry amongst all classes of people. In the state of Indiana, in which there is but one town that is of six years standing, there are several Book-clubs. Newspapers and Reviews from Philadelphia, Baltimore, Kentucky, and St. Louis, are received weekly.

— Document No. 8 —

LAND SALES AND CLAIM ASSOCIATIONS ON THE MIDDLEWESTERN FRONTIER[8]

Although the frontier environment modified the characteristics and traits of individuals under its influence, it failed to lessen their greed. Western avariciousness was expressed in its most unpleasant form in the constant struggle between speculators and farmers for choice land. Everywhere in the Middle West during the 1830's and 1840's pioneers attempted to appropriate the best acreage for themselves by "squatting," or simply occupying a plot until they could raise the money necessary for its purchase. When land jobbers, recognizing a chance to secure sites whose value had been increased by the frontiersmen's labors, tried to outbid the occupants at the regular government auctions, bitter conflicts often resulted. Usually the settlers attempted to meet the situation by forming "Claim Associations" whose members were pledged to deal harshly with speculators attempting to secure occupied land. An Iowa pioneer and writer, John B. Newhall, described these conflicts in one of his well-used guide books.

✦   ✦   ✦

This [squatting] may be considered a mode of settlement peculiar to that portion of the public domain which is occupied prior to its being surveyed by the general government. By mutual concession and an honorable adherence to neighborhood regulations, it has become a "pro tem" law, answering the purposes of general pro-

[8] John B. Newhall, *Sketches of Iowa, or the Emigrant's Guide* (New York, 1841), pp. 54-58.

tection for the homes of the settler until his land comes
into market. So general has this usage become, and so
united are the interests of the settlers, that it would be
deemed extremely hazardous, as well as highly dishonor-
able, for a speculator or stranger to *bid* upon their
"claims," even though they were *not* protected in a "pre-
emption right." It being clearly understood what improvement constitutes a "claim," and the settler conforming to
the requisitions of the "by-laws" of his neighborhood, or
township, it is just as much respected for the time being,
as if the occupant had the government patent for it. For
instance, an emigrant comes into the country, he looks
from county to county for a location. After having pleased
himself, he says, "I will make an improvement." He breaks
5 acres of ground, which holds his "claim" for 6 months;
or he builds a cabin 8 logs high with a roof, which is
equivalent to the ploughing, and holds it 6 months longer.
He then stakes out his half section of land, being a full
"claim," generally one quarter timber and one quarter
prairie; and thus his home is secure from trespass from
any one. If he chooses to sell his "claim," he is at perfect
liberty to do so, and the purchaser succeeds to all the right
and immunities of the first settler. . . .

In order to prevent unpleasant litigation, and to keep
up a spirit of harmony amongst neighbors, and the better
to protect them in their equitable rights of "claim" purchase, each township has its own organization generally
throughout the territory, and announces by public notice
a "call meeting," thus: "The citizens of township 72
north, range 5 west, are requested to meet at Squire
B————'s, Hickory Grove, (or as the place and
time may be) to adopt the necessary measures for securing
their homes at the approaching land sale at B————
or D————." After a short preamble and set of
resolutions, suited to the occasion, a "register" is appointed, whose duty it shall be to record the name of
each claimant to his respective "claim." A "bidder" is
also appointed, whose duty it shall be, on the day of
sale, to bid off all the land previously registered in the
name of each respective claimant. These associations are
formed mutually, to sustain and protect each other in
their claim-rights. Thus, every thing moves along at the

land sales with the harmony and regularity of clockwork; and should any one present be found bidding over the minimum price ($1.25,) on land registered in the township book, woe be unto him. Although "claim-law" is no law derived from the United States, or from the statute book of the territory, yet it nevertheless *is* the law, made by and derived from the sovereigns themselves, and its mandates are imperative.

When any controversy arises between two neighbors relative to trespassing, (in common parlance) "jumping a claim," it is arbitrated by a committee appointed for that purpose, and their decision is considered final. . . .

The great mass of people east of the Alleghanies, I apprehend, have but little idea of a western land sale. Many are the ominous indications of its approach among the "settlers." Every dollar is sacredly treasured up. The precious "mint drops" take to themselves wings, and fly away from the merchant's till to the farmer's cupboard. Times are dull in the towns; for the settler's home is dearer and *sweeter* than the merchant's sugar and coffee. At length the wished-for day arrives. The suburbs of the town present the scene of a military camp. The settlers have flocked from far and near. The hotels are thronged to overflowing. Barrooms, dining-rooms, and wagons, are metamorphosed into bedrooms. Dinners are eaten from a table or a stump; and thirst is quenched from a bar or a brook. The sale being announced from the land office, the township bidder stands near by with the registry book in hand, and each settler's name attached to his respective quarter or half section, and thus he bids off in the name of the whole township for each respective claimant. A thousand settlers are standing by, eagerly listening when *their* quarter shall be called off. The crier has passed the well-known numbers. His home is secure. He feels relieved. The litigation of "claim-jumping" is over forever. He is lord of the soil. With an independent step he walks into the land-office, opens the time-worn saddle-bags, and counts out the 200 or 400 dollars, silver and gold, takes his certificate from the general government, and goes his way rejoicing.

— Document No. 9 —

THE ORGANIZATION AND OPERATION OF THE SANTA FÉ TRADE[9]

As small farmers pushed their frontier across the Mississippi Valley, other pioneers were blazing new trails into the unknown lands beyond the Father of Waters. In the vanguard were the Santa Fé traders, whose giant caravans of covered wagons rolled westward each year after 1821, carrying Yankee textiles and hardware to trade with the merchants of the Mexican province of New Mexico. Their ventures not only stimulated the economy of the West but taught later overland "emigrants" the techniques of plains travel as well as demonstrating the weakness of Mexico's hold on its northern provinces. The manner in which the yearly caravan was organized for its journey near Independence, Missouri, and the beginning of its march were described in classic form by Josiah Gregg, himself a Santa Fé Trader, in his Commerce of the Prairies.

✓   ✓   ✓

The designation of "Council Grove," after all, is perhaps the most appropriate that could be given to this place; for we there held a "grand council," at which the respective claims of the different "aspirants to office" were considered, leaders selected, and a system of government agreed upon,—as is the standing custom of these promiscuous caravans. One would have supposed that electioneering and "party spirit" would hardly have penetrated so far into the wilderness: but so it was. Even in

[9] Josiah Gregg, *Commerce of the Prairies* (2 vols., New York, 1844), I, pp. 44-47, 50-53.

our little community we had our "officeseekers" and
their "political adherents," as earnest and as devoted as
any of the modern schools of politicians in the midst of
civilization. After a great deal of bickering and wordy
warfare, however, all the "candidates" found it expedient
to decline, and a gentleman by the name of Stanley, without seeking, or even desiring the "office" was unanimously
proclaimed "Captain of the Caravan." The powers of this
officer were undefined by any "constitutional provision,"
and consequently vague and uncertain: orders being only
viewed as mere requests, they are often obeyed or neglected at the caprice of the subordinates. It is necessary
to observe, however, that the captain is expected to
direct the order of travel during the day, and to designate
the camping-ground at night; with many other functions
of a general character, in the exercise of which the company find it convenient to acquiesce. But the little attention that is paid to his commands in cases of emergency,
I will leave the reader to become acquainted with,
as I did, by observing their manifestations during the
progress of the expedition.

But after this comes the principal task of organizing.
The proprieters are first notified by "proclamation" to
furnish a list of their men and wagons. The latter are
generally apportioned into four "divisions," particularly
when the company is large—and ours consisted of nearly
a hundred wagons, besides a dozen of dearborns and
other small vehicles, and two small cannons (a four and
six pounder), each mounted upon a carriage. To each
of these divisions, a "lieutenant" was appointed, whose
duty it was to inspect every ravine and creek on the
route, select the best crossings, and superintend what is
called in prairie parlance, the "forming" of each encampment.

Upon the calling of the roll, we were found to muster
an efficient force of nearly two hundred men without
counting invalids or other disabled bodies, who, as a
matter of course, are exempt from duty. There is nothing
so much dreaded by inexperienced travellers as the ordeal
of guard duty. But no matter what the condition or
employment of the individual may be, no one has the
smallest chance of evading the "common law of the

prairies." The amateur tourist and the listless loafer are precisely in the same wholesome predicament—they must all take their regular turn at the watch. There is usually a set of genteel idlers attached to every caravan, whose wits are for ever at work in devising schemes for whiling away their irksome hours at the expense of others. By embarking in these "trips of pleasure," they are enabled to live without expense; for the hospitable traders seldom refuse to accommodate even a loafing companion with a berth at their mess without charge. But then these lounging *attachés* are expected at least to do good service by way of guard duty. None are ever permitted to furnish a substitute, as is frequently done in military expeditions, for he that would undertake to stand the tour of another besides his own, would scarcely be watchful enough for the dangers of the Prairies. Even the invalid must be able to produce unequivocal proofs of his inability, or it is a chance if the plea is admitted. For my own part, although I started on the "sick list," and though the prairie sentinel must stand fast and brook the severest storm (for then it is that the strictest watch is necessary), I do not remember ever having missed my post but once during the whole journey. . . .

The familiar note of preparation, "Catch up! catch up!" was now sounded from the captain's camp, and re-echoed from every division and scattered group along the valley. On such occasions, a scene of confusion ensues, which must be seen to be appreciated. The woods and dales resound with the gleeful yells of the light-hearted wagoners, who, weary of inaction, and filled with joy at the prospect of getting under way, become clamorous in the extreme. Scarcely does the jockey on the race-course ply his whip more promptly at that magic word "Go," than do these emulous wagoners fly to harnessing their mules at the spirit-stirring sound of "Catch up." Each teamster vies with his fellow who shall be soonest ready; and it is a matter of boastful pride to be the first to cry out—"All's set!"

The uproarious bustle which follows—the hallooing of those in pursuit of animals—the exclamations which the unruly brutes call forth from their wrathful drivers; together with the clatter of bells—the rattle of yokes and harness—the jingle of chains—all conspire to produce an uproarious confusion, which would be altogether imcomprehensible without the assistance of the eyes; while these alone would hardly suffice to unravel the labyrinthian manoeuvres and hurly-burly of this precipitate breaking up. It is sometimes amusing to observe the athletic wagoner hurrying an animal to its post—to see him "heave upon" the halter of a stubborn mule, while the brute as obstinately "sets back," determined not to "move a peg" till his own good pleasure thinks it proper to do so—his whole manner seeming to say, 'Wait till your hurry's over!" I have more than once seen a driver hitch a harnessed animal to the halter, and by that process haul "his mulishness" forward, while each of his four projected feet would leave a furrow behind; until at last the perplexed master would wrathfully exclaim, "A mule will be a mule any way you can fix it!"

"All's set!" is finally heard from some teamster—"All's set," is directly responded from every quarter. "Stretch out!" immediately vociferates the captain. Then, the "heps!" of drivers—the cracking of whips—the trampling of feet—the occasional creak of wheels—the rumbling of wagons—form a new scene of exquisite confusion, which I shall not attempt further to describe. "Fall in!" is heard from head-quarters, and the wagons are forthwith strung out upon the long inclined plain, which stretches to the heights beyond Council Grove.

After fifteen miles' progress, we arrived at the "Diamond Spring" (a crystal fountain discharging itself into a small brook), to which, in later years, caravans have sometimes advanced, before "organizing." Near twenty-five miles beyond we crossed the Cottonwood fork of the Neosho, a creek still smaller than that of Council Grove, and our camp was pitched immediately in its further valley.

When caravans are able to cross in the evening, they seldom stop on the near side of a stream—first, because if it happens to rain during the night, it may become flooded, and cause both detention and trouble: again, though the stream be not impassable after rain, the banks become slippery and difficult to ascend. A third and still more important reason is, that, even supposing the contingency of rain does not occur, teams will rarely pull as well in "cold collars," as wagoners term it—that is, when fresh geared—as in the progress of a day's travel. When a heavy pull is just at hand in the morning, wagoners sometimes resort to the expedient of driving a circuit upon the prairie, before venturing to "take the bank."

— Document No. 10 —

THE ROLE OF THE MOUNTAIN MEN IN OPENING THE FAR WEST[10]

More important than the Santa Fé traders in opening the trans-Mississippi West to settlers were the fur trappers who roamed the Rocky Mountain country and the deserts of the Great Basin between the 1820's and the 1840's. During those two decades some six hundred of these Mountain Men lived continuously in the West, exploring constantly for untrapped beaver streams, and in so doing unlocking the geographical secrets of that vast domain. Once each year they renewed their contacts with civilization when they met a trading caravan from St. Louis at a designated "rendezvous" where fresh supplies were purchased and the profits accumulated in twelve months of dangerous hunting dissipated in a few weeks of wild revelry. George F. Ruxton, an English traveler and novelist who lived among the fur trappers of the upper Arkansas River during the winter and spring of 1847, penned a vivid account of their way of life as it developed under the corroding influence of the wilderness.

[10] George F. Ruxton, *Adventures in Mexico and the Rocky Mountains* (London, 1849), pp. 241-246.

The trappers of the Rocky Mountains belong to a "genus" more approximating to the primitive savage than perhaps any other class of civilized man. Their lives being spent in the remote wilderness of the mountains, with no other companion than Nature herself, their habits and character assume a most singular cast of simplicity mingled with ferocity, appearing to take their colouring from the scenes and objects which surround them. Knowing no wants save those of nature, their sole care is to procure sufficient food to support life, and the necessary clothing to protect them from the rigorous climate. This, with the assistance of their trusty rifles, they are generally able to effect, but sometimes at the expense of great peril and hardship. When engaged in their avocation, the natural instinct of primitive man is ever alive, for the purpose of guarding against danger and the provision of necessary food.

Keen observers of nature, they rival the beasts of prey in discovering the haunts and habits of game, and in their skill and cunning in capturing it. Constantly exposed to perils of all kinds, they become callous to any feeling of danger, and destroy human as well as animal life with as little scruple and as freely as they expose their own. Of laws, human or divine, they neither know nor care to know. Their wish is their law, and to attain it they do not scruple as to ways and means. Firm friends and bitter enemies, with them it is "a word and a blow," and the blow often first. They may have good qualities, but they are those of the animal; and people fond of giving hard names call them revengeful, bloodthirsty, drunkards (when the wherewithal is to be had), gamblers, regardless of the laws of *meum* and *tuum*—in fact, "White Indians." However, there are exceptions, and I *have* met honest mountain-men. Their animal qualities, however, are undeniable. Strong, active, hardy as bears, daring, expert in the use of their weapons, they are just what uncivilised white man might be supposed to be in a brute state, depending upon his instinct for the support of life. Not a hole or corner in the vast wilderness of the "Far West" but has been ransacked by these hardy men. From the Mississippi to the mouth of the Colorado of the West, from the frozen regions of the North to the Gila in Mexico, the beaver-hunter has set his traps in every creek and stream. All this vast country, but for the daring enterprise of these men, would be even now a *terra incognita* to geographers, as indeed a great portion still is; but there is not an acre that has not been passed and repassed by the trappers in their perilous excursions. The mountains and streams still retain the names assigned to them by the rude hunters; and these alone are the hardy pioneers who have paved the way for the settlement of the western country.

Trappers are of two kinds, the "hired hand" and the "free trapper": the former hired for the hunt by the fur companies; the latter, supplied with animals and traps by the company, is paid a certain price for his furs and peltries.

There is also the trapper "on his own hook"; but this class is very small. He has his own animals and traps, hunts where he chooses, and sells his peltries to whom he pleases.

On starting for a hunt, the trapper fits himself out with the necessary equipment, either from the Indian trading-forts, or from some of the petty traders—coureurs des bois—who frequent the western country. This equipment consists usually of two or three horses or mules—one for saddle, the others for packs—and six traps, which are carried in a bag of leather called a *trap-sack*. Ammunition, a few pounds of tobacco, dressed deer-skins for mocassins, &c., are carried in a wallet of dressed buffalo-skin, called a possible-sack. His "possibles" and "trap-sack" are generally carried on the saddle-mule when hunting, the others being packed with the furs. The costume of the trapper is a hunting-shirt of dressed buckskin, ornamented with long fringes; pantaloons of the same material, and decorated with porcupine quills and long fringes down the outside of the leg. A flexible felt hat and mocassins clothe his extremities. Over his left shoulder and under his right arm hang his powder-horn and bullet-pouch, in which he carries his balls, flint and steel, and odds and ends of all kinds. Round the waist is a belt, in which is stuck a large butcher-knife in a sheath of buffalo-hide, made fast to the belt by a chain or guard of steel; which also supports a little buckskin case containing a whetstone. A tomahawk is also often added; and, of course, a long heavy rifle is part and parcel of his equipment. I had nearly forgotten the pipe-holder, which hangs around his neck, and is generally a *gage d'amour,* and a triumph of squaw workmanship, in shape of a heart, garnished with beads and porcupine-quills.

Thus provided, and having determined the locality of his trapping-ground, he starts to the mountains, sometimes alone, sometimes with three or four in company, as soon as the breaking up of the ice allows him to commence operations. Arrived on his hunting-grounds, he follows the creeks and streams, keeping a sharp look-out for "sign." If he sees a prostrate cotton-wood tree, he examines it to discover if it be the work of beaver—whether "thrown" for the purpose of food, or to dam the stream. The track of the beaver on the mud or sand under the bank is also examined; and if the "sign" be fresh, he sets his trap in the run of the animal, hiding it under water, and attaching it by a stout chain to a picket driven in the bank, or to a bush or tree. A "float-stick" is made fast to the trap by a cord a few feet long, which, if the animal carry away the trap, floats on the water and points out its position. The trap is baited with the "medicine," an oily substance obtained from a gland in the scrotum of the beaver, but distinct from the testes. A stick is dipped into this and planted over the trap; and the beaver, attracted by the smell, and wishing a close inspection, very foolishly puts his leg into the trap, and is a "gone beaver."

When a lodge is discovered, the trap is set at the edge of the dam, at the point where the animal passes from deep to shoal water, and always under water. Early in the morning the hunter mounts his mule and examines the traps. The captured animals are skinned, and the tails, which are a great dainty, carefully packed into camp. The skin is then stretched over a hoop or framework of osier-twigs, and is allowed to dry, the flesh and fatty substance being carefully scraped (grained). When dry, it is folded into a square sheet, the fur turned inwards, and the bundle, containing about ten to twenty skins, tightly pressed and corded, and is ready for transportation.

During the hunt, regardless of Indian vicinity, the fearless trapper wanders far and near in search of "sign." His nerves must ever be in a state of tension, and his mind ever present at his call. His eagle eye sweeps round the country, and in an instant detects any foreign appearance. A turned leaf, a blade of grass pressed down, the uneasiness of the wild animals, the flight of birds, are all paragraphs to him written in nature's legible hand and plainest language. All the wits of the subtle savage are called into play to gain an advantage over the wily woodsman; but with the natural instinct of primitive man, the white hunter has the advantages of a civilised mind, and, thus provided, seldom fails to outwit, under equal advantages, the cunning savage.

Sometimes, following on his trail, the Indian watches him set his traps on a shrub-belted stream, and, passing up the bed, like Bruce of old, so that he may leave no track, he lies in wait in the bushes until the hunter comes to examine his carefully-set traps. Then, waiting until he approaches his ambushment within a few feet, whiz flies the home-drawn arrow, never failing at such close quarters to bring the victim to the ground. For one white scalp, however, that dangles in the smoke of an Indian's lodge, a dozen black ones, at the end of the hunt, ornament the camp-fires of the "rendezvous."

At a certain time, when the hunt is over, or they have loaded their pack-animals, the trappers proceed to the "rendezvous," the locality of which has been previously agreed upon; and here the traders and agents of the fur companies await them, with such assortment of good as their hardy customers may require, including generally a fair supply of alcohol. The trappers drop in singly and in small bands, bringing their packs of beaver to this mountain market, not unfrequently to the value of a thousand dollars each, the produce of one hunt. The dissipation of the "rendezvous," however, soon turns the trapper's pocket inside out. The goods brought by the traders, although of the most inferior quality, are sold at enormous prices:—Coffee, twenty and thirty shillings a pint-cup, which is the usual measure; tobacco fetches ten and fifteen shillings a plug; alcohol, from twenty to fifty shillings a pint; gunpowder, sixteen shillings a pint-cup; and all other articles at proportionately exorbitant prices.

The "beaver" is purchased at from two to eight dollars per pound; the Hudson's Bay Company alone buying it by the pluie, or "plew," that is, the whole skin, giving a certain price for skins, whether of old beaver or "kittens."

The "rendezvous" is one continued scene of drunkenness, gambling, and brawling and fighting, as long as the money and credit of the trappers last. Seated, Indian fashion, round the fires, with a blanket spread before them, groups are seen with their "decks" of cards, playing at "euker," "poker," and "seven-up," the regular mountain games. The stakes are "beaver," which here is current coin; and when the fur is gone, their horses, mules, rifles, and shirts, hunting-packs, and *breeches,* are staked. Daring gamblers make the rounds of the camp, challenging each other to play for the trapper's highest stake,—his horse, his squaw (if he have one), and, as once happened, his scalp. There goes "hos and beaver!" is the mountain expression when any great loss is sustained; and, sooner or later, "hos and beaver" invariably find their way into the insatiable pockets of the traders. A trapper often squanders the produce of his hunt, amounting to hundreds of dollars, in a couple of hours; and, supplied on credit with another equipment, leaves the "rendezvous" for another expedition, which has the same result time after time; although one tolerably successful hunt would enable him to return to the settlements and civilised life, with an ample sum to purchase and stock a farm, and enjoy himself in ease and comfort the remainder of his days.

An old trapper, a French Canadian, assured me that he had received fifteen thousand dollars for beaver during a sojourn of twenty years in the mountains. Every year he resolved in his mind to return to Canada, and, with this object, always converted his fur into cash; but a fortnight at the "rendezvous" always cleaned him out, and, at the end of twenty years, he had not even credit sufficient to buy a pound of powder.

These annual gatherings are often the scene of bloody duels, for over their cups and cards no men are more quarrelsome than your mountaineers. Rifles, at twenty paces, settle all differences, and, as may be imagined, the fall of one or other of the combatants is certain, or, as sometimes happens, both fall to the word "fire."

— Document No. 11 —

THE PEOPLING OF THE TEXAS FRONTIER[11]

The traders and trappers who explored and advertised the Far West set the tide of population flowing there. One objective of the pioneers was the black-soil area of the Mexican province of Texas, which was formally opened to Americans in 1821 by Moses and Stephen Austin, two Americans who obtained a government land grant there. Fifteen years later the newcomers were sufficiently numerous to stage the revolution that separated the Republic of Texas from Mexico and eventually added it to the United States. Conditions on this unique frontier were described by a visitor, Mary A. Holley, in a letter written from Bolivar, Texas, in December, 1831, together with a plea for strong, adventurous settlers to build up the country.

✓   ✓   ✓

Ones feelings in Texas are unique and original, and very like a dream or youthful vision realized. Here, as in Eden, man feels alone with the God of nature, and seems, in a peculiar manner, to enjoy the rich bounties of heaven, in common with all created things. The animals, which do not fly from him; the profound stillness; the genial sun and soft air,—all are impressive, and are calculated, both

[11] Mary A. Holley, *Texas* (Baltimore, 1833), pp. 127-131.

to delight the imagination, and to fill the heart, with religious emotions.

With regard to the state of society here, as is natural to expect, there are many incongruities. It will take some time for people gathered from the north, and from the south, from the east, and from the west, to assimilate, and adapt themselves to new situations. The people are universally kind and hospitable, which are redeeming qualities. Everybody's house is open, and table spread, to accommodate the traveller. There are no poor people here, and none rich; that is, none who have much money. The poor and the rich, to use the correlatives, where distinction, there is none, get the same quantity of land on arrival, and if they do not continue equal, it is for want of good management on the one part, or superior industry and sagacity on the other. All are happy, because busy; and none meddle with the affairs of their neighbours, because they have enough to do to take care of their own. They are bound together by a common interest, by sameness of purpose, and hopes. As far as I could learn, they have no envyings, no jealousies, no bickerings, through politics or fanaticism. There is neither masonry, antimasonry, nullification nor court intrigues.

The common concerns of life are sufficiently exciting to keep the spirits buoyant, and prevent everything like ennui. Artificial wants are entirely forgotten, in the view of real ones, and self, eternal self, does not alone, fill up the round of life. Delicate ladies find they can be useful, and need not be vain. Even privations become pleasures: people grow ingenious in overcoming difficulties. Many latent faculties are developed. They discover in themselves, powers, they did not suspect themselves of possessing. Equally surprised and delighted at the discovery, they apply to their labours with all that energy and spirit, which new hope and conscious strength, inspire.

You wish to know my opinion, if it will do for all sorts of people to emigrate to Texas, and if I would advise J————— and S————— to sell out and remove. On this point, I should say, industrious farmers will certainly do well, and cannot fail of success; that is to say, if abundant crops, and a ready market with high prices, will satisfy them. Substantial planters, with capital and hands, may enlarge their operations here to any extent, and with enormous profits. One gentleman, for instance, whom I visited, has ninety-three acres under cultivation, by seven hands. His crop, this year, consists of eighty bales of cotton, two thousand bushels of corn, five hundred bushels of sweet potatoes, besides other articles of minor importance.

Those persons, however, who are established in comfort and competency, with an ordinary portion of domestic happiness; who have never been far from home, and are excessively attached to personal ease; who shrink from hardship and danger, and those who, being accustomed to a regular routine of prescribed employment in a city, know not how to act on emergencies, or adapt themselves to all sorts of circumstances, had better stay where they are. There is no better advice, than, "to let well enough alone." All changes may be for the worse as well as better, and what we are used to, though not so good as might be, may suit us best. New shoes, though handsomer and better than old ones, may pinch and fret the wearer. Happiness is relative. A high standard for one person, is a low one for another, and what one prizes, another may think worthless. So that even conceding all the advantages I have claimed for Texas, it does not follow that the happiness of all would be promoted, by emigrating to this country. It depends much upon the spirit of the man.

He whose hopes of rising to independence in life, by honourable exertion, have been blasted by disappointment; whose ambition has been thwarted by untoward circumstances; whose spirit, though depressed, is not discouraged; who longs only for some ample field on which to lay out his strength; who does not hanker after society nor sigh for the vanished illusions of life; who has a fund of resources within himself, and a heart to trust in God and his own exertions; who is not peculiarly sensitive to petty inconveniences, but can bear privations and make sacrifices, of personal comfort—such a person will do well to settle accounts at home, and begin life anew in Texas. He will find, here, abundant exercise for all his faculties, both of body and mind, a new stimulus to his exertions, and a new current for his affections. He may be obliged to labour hard, but riches are a very certain reward of his exertions. He may be generous, without fear of ruin. He will learn to find society in nature, and repose in solitude, health in exertion, and happiness in occupation. If he have a just ambition, he will glow with generous pride, while he is marking out an untrodden path, acting in an unhackneyed sphere, and founding for himself, and his children after him, a permanent and noble independence.

— Document No. 12 —

THE SPREAD OF THE "OREGON FEVER"[12]

While some pioneers were wresting Texas from its Mexican owners, others were plodding westward along the rugged trail that led to the Oregon country. Claimed jointly by the United States and England, this fertile land was well advertised by both the fur trappers and by missionaries who settled there during the 1830's. As their tales of the richness of the Willamette Valley of Oregon circulated throughout the Mississippi Valley, thousands upon thousands of persons were infected with the "Oregon Fever." Each year, beginning in 1841, victims of this malady sold their farms, converted wagons into "prairie schooners," and made their way to Independence, Missouri, the jumping-off point for the journey across the plains. The editor of the Missouri Expositor, *watching the fever rage among his countrymen, described the excitement that prevailed everywhere.*

[12] *Niles' National Register,* May 21, 1845, quoting the *Missouri Expositor,* May 3, 1845, p. 203.

Even while we write, we see a long train of wagons coming through our busy streets; they are hailed with shouts of welcome by their fellow voyagers, and, to judge from the pleased expression on every face, it "all goes merry as a marriage bell." On looking out at the passing train, we see among the foremost a very comfortably covered wagon, one of the sheets drawn aside, and an extremely nice looking lady seated inside very quietly sewing; the bottom of the wagon is carpeted; there are two or three chairs, and at one end there is a bureau, surmounted by a mirror; various articles of ornament and convenience hang around the sides—a perfect prairie boudoir. Blessed be woman! Shedding light and happiness where'er she goes; with her the wild prairie will be a paradise! Blessed be him who gave us this connecting link between heaven and man to win us from our wilder ways. Hold on there; this is getting entirely too sentimental; but we don't care who laughs, we felt better and happier when we looked on this picture than we may express. That fine manly fellow riding along by the side of the wagon, and looking in so pleasantly, is doubtless the lady's husband; we almost envy him. But they are past, and now comes team after team, each drawn by six or eight stout oxen, and such drivers! positively sons of Anak! not one of them less than six feet two in his stockings. Whoo ha! Go it boys! We're in perfect *Oregon fever*. Now comes on a stock of every description; children, niggers, horses, mules, cows, oxen; and there seems to be no end of them. From present evidences, we suppose that not less than two or three thousand people are congregating at this point previous to their start upon the broad prairie, which will be on or about the 10th of May.

— Document No. 13 —

LIFE ALONG THE OREGON TRAIL[13]

*As victims of the Oregon Fever flocked into Inde-
pendence, they formed caravans for the journey across
the plains. Then, with an elected captain, lieutenants, and
"pilot" in charge, the march began. One of the largest
caravans made the journey in 1843, with nearly a thousand persons and five thousand cattle. After a few days
on the trail, the party divided, with some moving ahead
rapidly and others following more slowly with the live
stock. The captain of the latter group, the "cow column,"
was Jesse Applegate, who wrote a classic description of
life on the road to Oregon.*

It is four o'clock A.M.; the sentinels on duty have
discharged their rifles—the signal that the hours of sleep
are over; and every wagon and tent is pouring forth its
night tenants, and slow-kindling smokes begin largely to
rise and float away on the morning air. Sixty men start
from the corral, spreading as they make through the vast
herd of cattle and horses that form a semi-circle around
the encampment, the most distant perhaps two miles
away.

The herders pass to the extreme verge and carefully
examine for trails beyond, to see that none of the animals
have strayed or been stolen during the night. This morning no trails lead beyond the outside animals in sight, and
by five o'clock the herders begin to contract the great mov-

[13] Jesse Applegate's "A Day with the Cow Column," was
first published in the *Transactions of the Fourth Annual Re-
union of the Oregon Pioneer Association for 1876* (Salem,
Oregon, 1877). An excellent modern editon is Jesse Applegate, *A Day with the Cow Column* (Chicago, 1934), from
which the account above is quoted, pp. 5-17.

ing circle and the well-trained animals move slowly toward camp, clipping here and there a thistle or tempting bunch of grass on the way. In about an hour five thousand animals are close up to the encampment, and the teamsters are busy selecting their teams and driving them inside the "corral" to be yoked. The corral is a circle one hundred yards deep, formed with wagons connected strongly with each other, the wagon in the rear being connected with the wagon in front by its tongue and ox chains. It is a strong barrier that the most vicious ox cannot break, and in case of an attack of the Sioux would be no contemptible entrenchment.

From six to seven o'clock is a busy time; breakfast is to be eaten, the tents struck, the wagons loaded, and the teams yoked and brought up in readiness to be attached to their respective wagons. All know when, at seven o'clock, the signal to march sounds, that those not ready to take their proper places in the line of march must fall into the dusty rear for the day.

There are sixty wagons. They have been divided into fifteen divisions or platoons of four wagons each, and each platoon is entitled to lead in its turn. The leading platoon of today will be the rear one tomorrow, and will bring up the rear unless some teamster, through indolence or negligence, has lost his place in the line, and is condemned to that uncomfortable post. It is within ten minutes of seven; the corral but now a strong barricade is everywhere broken, the teams being attached to the wagons. The women and children have taken their places in them. The pilot (a borderer who has passed his life on the verge of civilization, and has been chosen to the post of leader from his knowledge of the savage and his experience in travel through roadless wastes) stands ready in the midst of his pioneers, and aids, to mount and lead the way. Ten or fifteen young men, not today on duty, form another cluster. They are ready to start on a buffalo hunt, are well mounted, and well armed as they need be, for the unfriendly Sioux have driven the buffalo out of the Platte, and the hunters must ride fifteen or twenty miles to reach them. The cow drivers are hastening, as they get ready, to the rear of their charge, to collect and prepare them for the day's march.

It is on the stroke of seven; the rushing to and fro, the cracking of the whips, the loud command to oxen, and what seems to be the inextricable confusion of the last ten minutes has ceased. Fortunately every one has been found and every teamster is at his post. The clear notes of the trumpet sound in the front; the pilot and his guards mount their horses, the leading division of wagons moves out of the encampment, and takes up the line of march, the rest fall into their places with the precision of clock work, until the spot so lately full of life sinks back into that solitude that seems to reign over the broad plain and rushing river as the caravan draws its lazy length toward the distant El Dorado. . . .

The caravan has been about two hours in motion and is now extended as widely as a prudent regard for safety will permit. First, near the bank of the shining river, is a company of horsemen; they seem to have found an obstruction, for the main body has halted while three or four ride rapidly along the bank of the creek or slough. They are hunting a favorable crossing for the wagons; while we look they have succeeded; it has apparently required no work to make it passable, for all but one of the party have passed on and he has raised a flag, no doubt a signal to the wagons to steer their course to where he stands. The leading teamster sees him though he is yet two miles off, and steers his course directly towards him, all the wagons following in his track. They (the wagons) form a line three quarters of a mile in length; some of the teamsters ride upon the front of their wagons, some walk beside their teams; scattered along the line companies of women and children are taking exercise on foot; they gather bouquets of rare and beautiful flowers that line the way; near them stalks a stately greyhound or an Irish wolf dog, apparently proud of keeping watch and ward over his master's wife and children.

Next comes a band of horses; two or three men or boys follow them, the docile and sagacious animals scarce needing this attention, for they have learned to follow in the rear of the wagons, and know that at noon they will be allowed to graze and rest. Their knowledge of time seems as accurate as of the place they are to occupy in the line, and even a full-blown thistle will scarcely tempt them to straggle or halt until the dinner hour has arrived. Not so with the large herd of horned beasts that bring up the rear; lazy, selfish and unsocial, it has been a task to get them in motion, the strong always ready to domineer over the weak, halt in the front and forbid the weaker to pass them. They seem to move only in fear of the driver's whip; though in the morning full to repletion, they have not been driven an hour before their hunger and thirst seem to indicate a fast of days' duration. Through all the long day their greed is never sated nor their thirst quenched, nor is there a moment of relaxation of the tedious and vexatious labors of their drivers, although to all others the march furnishes some season of relaxation or enjoyment. For the cow-drivers there is none. . . .

The pilot, by measuring the ground and timing the speed of the wagons and the walk of his horses, has determined the rate of each, so as to enable him to select the nooning place, as nearly as the requisite grass and water can be had at the end of five hours' travel of the wagons. Today, the ground being favorable, little time has been lost in preparing the road, so that he and his pioneers are at the nooning place an hour in advance of the wagons, which time is spent in preparing convenient watering places for the animals and digging little wells near the bank of the Platte. As the teams are not unyoked, but simply turned loose from the wagons, a corral is not formed at noon, but the wagons are drawn up in columns, four abreast, the leading wagon of each platoon on the left—the platoons being formed with that view. This brings friends together at noon as well as at night.

Today an extra session of the Council is being held, to settle a dispute that does not admit of delay, between a proprietor and a young man who has undertaken to do a man's service on the journey for bed and board. Many such engagements exist and much interest is taken in the manner this high court, from which there is no appeal, will define the rights of each party in such engagements. The Council was a high court in the most exalted sense. It was a Senate composed of the ablest and most respected fathers of the emigration. It exercised both legislative and judicial powers, and its laws and decisions proved it equal [to] and worthy of the high trust reposed in it. Its sessions were usually held on days when the caravan was not moving. It first took the state of the little commonwealth into consideration; revised or repealed rules defective or obsolete, and exacted such others as the exigencies seemed to require. The commonwealth being cared for, it next resolved itself into a court, to hear and settle private disputes and grievances. The offender and aggrieved appeared before it, witnesses were examined, and the parties were heard by themselves and sometimes by counsel. The judges thus being made fully acquainted with the case, and being in no way influenced or cramped by technicalities, decided all cases according to their merits. There was but little use for lawyers before this court, for no plea was entertained which was calculated to defeat the ends of justice. Many of these judges have since won honors in higher spheres. They have aided to establish on the broad basis of right and universal liberty two of the pillars of our great Republic in the Occident. Some of the young men who appeared before them as advocates have themselves sat upon the highest judicial tribunals, commanded armies, been Governors of States, and taken high positions in the Senate of the nation.

It is now one o'clock; the bugle has sounded, and the caravan has resumed its westward journey. It is in the same order, but the evening is far less animated than the morning march; a drowsiness has fallen apparently on man and beast; teamsters drop asleep on their perches and even walking by their teams, and the words of command are now addressed to the slowly creeping oxen in the softened tenor of women or the piping treble of children, while the snores of teamsters make a droning accompaniment. . . .

The sun is now getting low in the west, and at length the painstaking pilot is standing ready to conduct the train in the circle which he has previously measured and marked out, which is to form the invariable fortification for the night. The leading wagons follow him so nearly round the circle, that but a wagon length separates them. Each wagon follows in its track, the rear closing on the front until its tongue and ox chains will perfectly reach from one to the other, and so accurate the measurement and perfect the practice, that the hindmost wagon of the train always precisely closes the gateway. As each wagon is brought into position it is dropped from its team (the teams being inside the circle), the team un-yoked, and the yokes and chains are used to connect the wagon strongly with that in its front. Within ten minutes from the time the leading wagon halted, the barricade is formed, the teams unyoked and driven out to pasture.

Everyone is busy preparing fires of buffalo chips to cook the evening meal, pitching tents and otherwise preparing for the night.

— Document No. 14 —

THE ATTACK ON SONOMA BY CALIFORNIA'S BEAR FLAGGERS[14]

Just as American migration into the Oregon country helped win that region for the United States in the 1846 settlement with Britain, so also did a parallel influx into California contribute to the acquisition of that rich do-main. The California trail was opened in 1841, and five years later about one thousand frontiersmen lived in the Sacramento Valley, all of them openly hostile to their Mexican overlords. When the arrival of the explorer, John C. Frémont, with sixty stout followers, gave them courage, a band of the more reckless malcontents first seized a herd of horses belonging to Mexican officials, then determined to capture General Mariano G. Vallejo, an influential Mexican-Californian. After an all night ride in June, 1846, they reached his home in Sonoma just at

[14] Simeon Ide, *A Biographical Sketch of the Life of William B. Ide* (n.p., 1880), pp. 123-128.

daybreak. The scene that followed, which launched the Bear Flag Revolt, was described by one of the participants, William B. Ide.

✓ ✓ ✓

Thus circumstanced, we arrived at Sonoma; and, after reconnoitering the place, and notifying our friends of our object in seizing the aforesaid gentlemen, and having secured the captain of the guard whom we found a little way out of town, we surrounded the house of Gen. M. G. Vallejo just at daybreak, on the 14th. William Merritt, Doct. Semple and Mr. Knight, (who took wise care to have it understood on all hands that he was forced into the scrape as an interpreter), entered the house to secure their prisoners.

Jacob P. Leese, an American by birth, and brother-in-law of Gen. Vallejo, who lived near by, was soon there, to soothe the fears, and otherwise as far as possible assist his friends. Doct. Salvadore was also found there, and Col. Prudshon was also soon arrested and brought there. After the first surprise had a little subsided, as no immediate violence was offered, the General's generous *spirits* gave proof of his usual hospitality—as the richest wines and brandies sparkled in the glasses, and those who had thus unceremoniously met soon became merry companions; more especially—the weary visitors.

While matters were going on thus happily in the house, the main force sat patiently guarding it without. They appeared to understand that they had performed all the duty required of them, and only waited, that the said prisoners might be prepared and brought forth for their journey, and—waited still. The sun was climbing up the heavens an hour or more, and yet no man, nor voice, nor sound of violence came from the house to tell us of events within: patience was ill, and lingered ill. "Let us have a captain," said one—a *captain*, said all. Capt. Grigsby was elected, and went immediately into the house. The men still sat upon their horses—patience grew faint; an hour became an age. "Oh! go into the house, *Ide*, and come out again and let us know what is going on there!" No sooner said than done. There sat Doct. S., just modifying a long string of articles of capitulation.

There sat Merritt—his head fallen: there sat Knight, no longer able to interpret; and there sat the new made Captain, as mute as the seat he sat upon. The bottles had well nigh vanquished the captors. The Articles of Capitulation were seized hastily, read and thrown down again, and the men outside were soon informed of their contents. Pardon us, dear Doctor—we will not make an exposition. It is sufficient to say, that by the rule of opposition, they gave motion and energy to the waiting mass, and all that was necesary was to direct the torrent and guide the storm.

No one hitherto in authority had thought of seizing the fortress, or disarming its guard. Capt. Grigsby was hastily called, and the men demanded of him that the prisoners should be immediately conveyed to the Sacramento valley. Capt. G. inquired, "What are the orders of Capt. Frémont in relation to these men?" Each man looked on his fellow, yet none spake. "But have you not got Capt. Frémont's name in black and white to authorize you in this you have done?" cried the enraged Captain—and immediately we demanded, that if there were any one present who had orders from him, either written or verbal, he declare the same. All declared, one after another, that they had no such orders. Thereupon the Captain was briefly but particularly informed, that the people whom he knew had received from Gen. Castro, and others in authority, the most insolent indignities— had been, on pain of death, ordered to leave the country; and that they had resolved to take the redress of grievances into their own hands; that we could not claim the protection of any government on earth, and were alone responsible for our conduct; that—(Here the Captain's "fears of doing wrong" overcame his patriotism,) and he interrupted the speaker by saying, *"Gentlemen, I have been deceived; I cannot go with you; I resign and back out of the scrape.* I can take my family to the mountains as cheap as any of you"—and Doct. S. at that moment led him into the house. Disorder and confusion prevailed. One swore he would not stay to guard prisoners— another swore we would all have our throats cut—another called for fresh horses, and all were on the move —every man for himself; when the speaker [Mr. Ide] resumed his effort, raising his voice louder and more loud, as the men receded from the place, saying: "We need no horses; we want no horses. *Saddle no horse for me.* I can go to the Spaniards, and make FREEMEN of them. I will give myself to them. I will lay my bones here, before I will take upon myself the ignominy of commencing an honorable work, and then flee like cowards, like thieves, when no enemy is in sight. In vain will you say you had honorable motives! Who will believe it? *Flee this day, and the longest life cannot wear off your disgrace!* Choose ye! choose ye this day, what you will be! We are robbers, or we *must be conquerors!*"—and the speaker in despair turned his back upon his receding companions.

— Document No. 15 —

OVERLAND TRAILS TO THE GOLD FIELDS, 1849 [15]

Scarcely had the Mexican War added California and the Southwest to the United States when workmen deepening the mill race for a sawmill under construction for John A. Sutter on the American River made the discovery that touched off the greatest gold rush in history. For a time Californians or their neighbors from Oregon and Mexico monopolized the "diggings," but when President James K. Polk devoted a portion of his message to Congress in December, 1848, to the find, the whole nation suddenly caught fire with excitement. During the "rush of the Forty Niners" that followed nearly 100,000 would-be miners reached California, some of them by

[15] Bayard Taylor, *Eldorado; or, Adventures in the Path of Empire* (2 vols., London, 1850), II, pp. 36-41.

sea, via Panama or Cape Horn, but more over the overland trails. These were so crowded with the wagons of migrants that one caravan followed another only a few hundred yards apart. Bayard Taylor, a newspaper reporter who witnessed the rush, described the start from Independence.

✓   ✓   ✓

The great starting point for this route was Independence, Mo., where thousands were encamped through the month of April, waiting until the grass should be sufficiently high for their cattle, before they ventured on the broad ocean of the Plains. From the first of May to the first of June, company after company took its departure from the frontier of civilization, till the emigrant trail from Fort Leavenworth, on the Missouri, to Fort Laramie, at the foot of the Rocky Mountains, was one long line of mule-trains and wagons. The rich meadows of the Nebraska, or Platte, were settled for the time, and a single traveler could have journeyed for the space of a thousand miles, as certain of his lodging and regular meals as if he were riding through the old agricultural districts of the Middle States. The wandering tribes of Indians on the Plains—the Pawnees, Sioux and Arapahoes—were alarmed and bewildered by this strange apparition. They believed they were about to be swept away forever from their hunting-grounds and graves. As the season advanced and the great body of the emigrants got under way, they gradually withdrew from the vicinity of the trail and betook themselves to grounds which the former did not reach. All conflicts with them were thus avoided, and the emigrants passed the Plains with perfect immunity from their thievish and hostile visitations.

Another and more terrible scourge, however, was doomed to fall upon them. The cholera, ascending the Mississippi from New Orleans, reached St. Louis about the time of their departure from Independence, and overtook them before they were fairly embarked on the wilderness. The frequent rains of early spring, added to the hardship and exposure of their travel, prepared the way for its ravages, and the first three or four hundred miles of the trail were marked by graves. It is estimated that about four thousand persons perished from this cause. Men were seized without warning with the most violent symptoms, and instances occurred in which the sufferer was left to die alone by the road-side, while his panic-stricken companions pushed forward, vainly trusting to get beyond the influence of the epidemic. Rough boards were planted at the graves of those who were buried near the trail, but there are hundreds of others lying unmarked by any memorial, on the bleak surface of the open plain and among the barren depths of the mountains. I have heard men tell how they have gone aside from their company to bury some old and cherished friend—a brother, it may often have been—performing the last rites alone and unaided, and leaving the remains where none but the wolf will ever seek their resting-place.

By the time the companies reached Fort Laramie the epidemic had expended its violence, and in the pure air of the elevated mountain region they were safe from its further attacks. Now, however, the real hardships of their journey began. Up and down the mountains that hem in the Sweetwater Valley—over the spurs of the Wind River chain—through the Devil's Gate, and past the stupendous mass of Rock Independence—they toiled slowly up to the South Pass, descended to the tributaries of the Colorado and plunged into the rugged defiles of the Timpanozu Mountains. Here the pasturage became scarce and the companies were obliged to take separate trails in order to find sufficient grass for their teams. Many, who, in their anxiety to get forward with speed, had thrown away a great part of the supplies that encumbered them, now began to want, and were frequently reduced, in their necessity, to make use of their mules and horses for food. It was not unusual for a mess, by way of variety to the tough mule-meat, to kill a quantity of rattle-snakes, with which the mountains abounded, and have a dish of them fried, for supper. The distress of many of the emigrants might have been entirely avoided, had they possessed any correct idea, at the outset of the journey, of its length and privations.

It must have been a remarkable scene, which the City of the Great Salt Lake presented during the summer. There, a community of religious enthusiasts, numbering about ten thousand, had established themselves beside an inland sea, in a grand valley shut in by snow-capped mountains, a thousand miles from any other civilized spot, and were dreaming of rebuilding the Temple and creating a New Jerusalem. Without this resting place in mid-journey, the sufferings of the emigrants must have been much aggravated. The Mormons, however, whose rich grain-lands in the Valley of the Utah River had produced them abundance of supplies, were able to spare sufficient for those whose stocks were exhausted. Two or three thousand, who arrived late in the season, remained in the Valley all winter, fearing to undertake the toilsome journey which still remained.

Those who set out for California had the worst yet in store for them. Crossing the alternate sandy wastes and rugged mountain chains of the Great Basin to the Valley of Humboldt's River, they were obliged to trust entirely to their worn and weary animals for reaching the Sierra Nevada before the winter snows. The grass was scarce and now fast drying up in the scorching heat of mid-summer. In the endeavor to hasten forward and get the first chance of pasture, many again committed the same mistake of throwing away their supplies. I was told of one man, who, with a refinement of malice and cruelty which it would be impossible to surpass, set fire to the meadows of dry grass, for the sole purpose, it was supposed, of retarding the progress of those who were behind and might else overtake him. A company of the emigrants, on the best horses which were to be obtained, pursued him and shot him from the saddle as he rode—a fate scarcely equal to his deserts.

The progress of the emigrants along the Valley of Humboldt's River is described as having been slow and toilsome in the extreme. The River, which lies entirely within the Great Basin,—whose waters, like those of the uplands of Central Asia, have no connexion with the sea—shrinks away towards the end of summer, and finally loses itself in the sand, at a place called the Sink. Here, the single trail across the Basin divides into three branches, and the emigrants, leaving the scanty meadows about the Sink, have before them an arid desert, varying from fifty to eighty miles in breadth, according to the route which they take.

Many companies, on arriving at this place, were obliged to stop and recruit their exhausted animals, though exposed to the danger of being detained there the whole winter, from the fall of snow on the Sierra Nevada. Another, and very large body of them, took the upper route to Lawson's Pass, which leads to the head of the Sacramento Valley; but the greater part, fortunately, chose the old traveled trails, leading to Bear Creek and Yuba, by way of Truckee River, and to the head-waters of the Rio Americano by way of Carson's River.

The two latter routes are the shortest and best. After leaving the Sink of Humboldt's River, and crossing a desert of about fifty miles in breadth, the emigrant reaches the streams which are fed from the Sierra Nevada, where he finds good grass and plenty of game. The passes are described as terribly rugged and precipitous, leading directly up the face of the great snowy ridge. As, however, they are not quite eight thousand feet above the sea, and are reached from a plateau of more than four thousand feet, the ascent is comparatively short; while, on the western side, more than a hundred miles of mountain country must be passed, before reaching the level of the Sacramento Valley. There are frequent passes in the Sierra Nevada which were never crossed before the summer of 1849. Some of the emigrants, diverging from the known trail, sought a road for themselves, and found their way down from the snows to the head waters of the Tuolumne, the Calaveras and Feather River. The eastern slope of the Sierra Nevada is but imperfectly explored. All the emigrants concurred in representing it to me as an abrupt and broken region, the higher peaks of barren granite, the valleys deep and narrow, yet in many places timbered with pine and cedar of immense growth.

After passing the dividing ridge,—the descent from which was rendered almost impossible by precipices and steeps of naked rock—about thirty miles of alternate cañons and divides lay between the emigrants and the nearest diggings. The steepness of the slopes of this range is hardly equalled by any other mountains in the world. The rivers seem to wind their way through the bottoms of chasms, and in many places it is impossible to get down to the water. The word cañon (meaning, in Spanish, a funnel,) has a peculiar adaptation to these cleft channels through which the rivers are poured. In getting down from the summit ridge the emigrants told me they were frequently obliged to take the oxen from the wagon and lower it with ropes; but for the sheer descents which followed, another plan was adopted. The wheels were all locked, and only one yoke of oxen left in front; a middling-sized pine was then cut down, and the butt fastened to the axle-tree, the branchy top dragging on the earth. The holding back of the oxen, the sliding of the locked wheels, and the resistance of the tree together formed an opposing power sufficient to admit of a slow descent; but it was necessary to observe great care lest the pace should be quickened, for the slightest start would have overcome the resistance and given oxen, wagon and tree together a momentum that would have landed them at the bottom in a very different condition.

— Document No. 16 —

HOW THE FORTY NINERS DUG THE GOLD[16]

The miners who survived the hardships of the trails spread themselves over the Mother Lode country, a hilly domain that stretched along the western flank of the Sierra Nevada Mountains for 150 miles. There they developed the mining techniques that allowed them to garner

[16] Louise A. K. Clappe's "Shirley Letters" were first printed in *The Pioneer: or California Monthly Magazine* during 1854 and 1855. They have been reproduced in several modern editions, the first being *The Shirley Letters from California Mines in 1851-52* (San Francisco, 1922). The extract is quoted from pp. 211-217 of this edition.

their harvest of "dust" and nuggets, using washing pans, cradles, and long-toms or sluice boxes to separate the heavy gold from sand or gravel found in the beds of streams, and later sinking shafts to deposits at bed-rock level. Their methods were observed and described by Louise A. K. Clappe, or "Dame Shirley" as she signed herself, in letters written during 1851 and 1852 from the Feather River Canyon mines.

✓ ✓ ✓

Our countrymen are the most discontented of mortals. They are always longing for big strikes. If a claim is paying them a steady income, by which, if they pleased, they could lay up more in a month than they could in a year at home, still they are dissatisfied, and in most cases will wander off in search of better diggings. There are hundreds now pursuing this foolish course, who, if they had stopped where they first camped, would now have been rich men. Sometimes a company of these wanderers will find itself upon a bar where a few pieces of the precious metal lie scattered upon the surface of the ground. Of course they immediately prospect it, which is accomplished by panning out a few basinfuls of the soil. If it pays, they claim the spot and build their shanties. The news spreads that wonderful diggings have been discovered at such a place. The monte-dealers—those worse than fiends—rush, vulture-like, upon the scene and erect a round tent, where, in gambling, drinking, swearing, and fighting, the *many* reproduce pandemonium in more than its original horror, while a *few* honestly and industriously commence digging for gold, and lo! as if a fairy's wand had been waved above the bar, a full-grown mining town hath sprung into existence.

But, first, let me explain to you the claiming system. As there are no state laws upon the subject, each mining community is permitted to make its own. Here they have decided that no man may claim an area of more than forty feet square. This he stakes off, and puts a notice upon it, to the effect that he holds it for mining purposes. If he does not choose to work it immediately, he is obliged to renew the notice every ten days, for, without this precaution, any other person has a right to "jump" it, that is, to take it from him. There are many ways of evading the above law. For instance, an individual can hold as many claims as he pleases if he keeps a man at work in each, for this workman represents the original owner. I am told, however, that the laborer himself can jump the claim of the very man who employs him, if he pleases to do so. This is seldom, if ever, done. The person who is willing to be hired generally prefers to receive the six dollars per diem, of which he is *sure* in any case, to running the risk of a claim not proving valuable. After all, the holding of claims by proxy is considered rather as a carrying out of the spirit of the law than as an evasion of it. But there are many ways of *really* outwitting this rule, though I cannot stop now to relate them, which give rise to innumerable arbitrations, and nearly every Sunday there is a miner's meeting connected with this subject.

Having got our gold-mines discovered and claimed, I will try to give you a faint idea of how they work them. Here, in the mountains, the labor of excavation is extremely difficult, on account of the immense rocks which form a large portion of the soil. Of course no man can work out a claim alone. For that reason, and also for the same that makes partnerships desirable, they congregate in companies of four or six, generally designating themselves by the name of the place from whence the majority of the members have emigrated; as, for example, the Illinois, Bunker Hill, Bay State, etc., companies. In many places the surface soil, or in mining phrase, the top dirt, pays when worked in a long-tom. This machine (I have never been able to discover the derivation of its name) is a trough, generally about twenty feet in length and eight inches in depth, formed of wood, with the exception of six feet at one end, called the "riddle" (query, why "riddle"?), which is made of sheet-iron perforated with holes about the size of a large marble. Underneath this colander-like portion of the long-tom is placed another trough, about ten feet long, the sides six inches, perhaps, in height, which, divided through the middle by a slender slat, is called the riffle-box. It takes several persons to manage properly a long-tom. Three or four men station themselves with spades at the head of the machine, while at the foot of it stands an individual armed "wid de

shovel an' de hoe." The spadesmen throw in large quantities of the precious dirt, which is washed down to the
riddle by a stream of water leading into the long-tom
through wooden gutters of sluices. When the soil reaches
the riddle, it is kept constantly in motion by the man
with the hoe. Of course, by this means, all the dirt and
gold escapes through the perforations into the riffle-box
below, one compartment of which is placed just beyond
the riffle. Most of the dirt washes over the sides of the
riffle-box, but the gold, being so astonishingly heavy, remains safely at the bottom of it. When the machine gets
too full of stones to be worked easily, the man whose
business it is to attend to them throws them out with his
shovel, looking carefully among them as he does so for
any pieces of gold which may have been too large to
pass through the holes of the riddle. I am sorry to say
that he generally loses his labor. At night they pan out the
gold which has been collected in the riffle-box during the
day. Many of the miners decline washing the top dirt at
all, but try to reach as quickly as possible the bed-rock,
where are found the richest deposits of gold. The river
is supposed to have formerly flowed over this bed-rock,
in the crevices of which it left, as it passed away, the
largest portions of the so eagerly sought for ore. The
group of mountains amidst which we are living is a spur
of the Sierra Nevada, and the bed-rock, which in this
vicinity is of slate, is said to run through the entire range,
lying, in distance varying from a few feet to eighty or
ninety, beneath the surface of the soil. On Indian Bar the
bed-rock falls in almost perpendicular benches, while at
Rich Bar, the friction of the river has formed it into
large, deep basins, in which the gold, instead of being
found, as you would naturally suppose, in the bottom of
it, lies, for the most part, just below the rim. A good-
natured individual bored *me,* and tired *himself,* in a hope-
less attempt to make me comprehend that this was only a
necessary consequence of the undercurrent of the water,
but with my usual stupidity upon such matters I got but
a vague idea from his scientific explanation, and certainly
shall not mystify *you* with my confused notions thereupon.

When a company wish to reach the bed-rock as quickly
as possible, they sink a shaft (which is nothing more nor

less than digging a well) until they "strike it." They then commence drifting coyote-holes, as they call them, in search of crevices, which, as I told you before, often pay immensely. These coyote-holes sometimes extend hundred of feet into the side of the hill. Of course they are obliged to use lights in working them. They generally proceed until the air is so impure as to extinguish the lights, when they return to the entrance of the excavation and commence another, perhaps close to it. When they think that a coyote-hole has been faithfully worked, they clean it up, which is done by scraping the surface of the bed-rock with a knife, lest by chance they have overlooked a crevice, and they are often richly rewarded for this precaution.

— Document No. 17 —

THE MINING RUSH TO THE COMSTOCK LODE COUNTRY[17]

By the middle 1850's all of California's mines had been appropriated, leaving thousands of prospectors without employment. Hopelessly infected with the gold fever, they began extending their endless search for precious metals over all the mountains and deserts of the West, making strike after strike as they did so. Each major find led to a frantic "rush"—to the Fraser River of British Columbia, the streams of Idaho and Montana, the Rocky Mountain country of Colorado, the desert lands of Arizona. Of these, none was more spectacular than that into the Washoe district of Nevada, for there in 1859 pros-

[17] J. Ross Browne, "A Peep at Washoe," *Harper's New Monthly Magazine,* XXII (January, 1861), pp. 154-157.

pectors discovered the richest of all finds, the Comstock Lode, on the slopes of Mount Davidson. The excitement attending this rush, and the crude mining camp of Virginia City which sprang up at the site, were described by a visiting journalist, J. Ross Browne.

✓　　　　　✓　　　　　✓

On a slope of mountains speckled with snow, sage-bushes, and mounds of upturned earth, without any apparent beginning or end, congruity or regard for the eternal fitness of things, lay outspread the wondrous city of Virginia.

Frame shanties, pitched together as if by accident; tents of canvas, of blankets, of brush, of potato-sacks and old shirts, with empty whisky barrels for chimneys; smoky hovels of mud and stone; coyote holes in the mountain-side forcibly seized and held by men; pits and shafts with smoke issuing from every crevice; piles of goods and rubbish on craggy points, in the hollows, on the rocks, in the mud, in the snow, every where, scattered broadcast in pell-mell confusion, as if the clouds had suddenly burst overhead and rained down the dregs of all the filmsy, rickety, filthy little hovels and rubbish of merchandise that had ever undergone the process of evaporation from the earth since the days of Noah. The intervals of space, which may or may not have been streets, were dotted over with human beings of such sort, variety, and numbers that the famous ant-hills of Africa were as nothing in the comparison. To say that they were rough, muddy, unkempt and unwashed, would be but faintly expressive of their actual appearance; they were all this by reason of exposure to the weather; but they seemed to have caught the very diabolical tint and grime of the whole place. Here and there, to be sure, a San Francisco dandy of the "boiled shirt" and "stove-pipe" pattern loomed up in proud consciousness of the triumphs of art under adverse circumstances; but they were merely peacocks in the barn-yard.

A fraction of the crowd, as we entered the precincts of the town, were engaged in a lawsuit relative to a question of title. The arguments used on both sides were empty whisky bottles, after the fashion of the *Basilinum,* or club law, which, according to Addison, prevailed in the colleges of learned men in former times. Several of the disputants had already been knocked down and convinced, and various others were freely shedding their blood in the cause of justice. Even the bull-terriers took an active part—or, at least, a very prominent part. The difficulty was about the ownership of a lot, which had been staked out by one party and "jumped" by another. Some two or three hundred disinterested observers stood by, enjoying the spectacle, several of them with their hands on their revolvers, to be ready in case of any serious issue; but these dangerous weapons are only used on great occasion—a refusal to drink, or some illegitimate trick at monte.

Upon fairly reaching what might be considered the centre of the town, it was interesting to observe the manners and customs of the place. Groups of keen speculators were huddled around the corners, in earnest consultation about the rise and fall of stocks; rough customers, with red and blue flannel shirts, were straggling in from the Flowery Diggings, the Desert, and other rich points, with specimens of croppings in their hands, or offering bargains in the "Rogers," the "Lady Bryant," the "Mammoth," the "Woolly Horse," and Heaven knows how many other valuable *leads,* at prices varying from ten to seventy-five dollars a foot. Small knots of the knowing ones were in confidential inter-change of thought on the subject of every other man's business; here and there a loose man was caught by the button, and led aside behind a shanty to be "stuffed"; everybody had some grand secret, which nobody else could find out; and the game of "dodge" and "pump" was universally played. Jew clothing-men were setting out their goods and chattels in front of wretched-looking tenements; monte-dealers, gamblers, thieves, cut-throats, and murderers were mingling miscellaneously in the dense crowds gathered around the bars of the drinking saloons. Now and then a half-starved Pah-Ute or Washoe Indian came tottering along under a heavy press of fagots and whisky. On the main street, where the mass of the population were gathered, a jaunty fellow who had "made a good thing of it" dashed through the crowds on horseback, accoutred in genuine Mexican style, swinging his *reata* over his head, and yelling like a devil let loose. All this time the wind blew in terrific gusts from the four quarters of the compass, tearing away signs, capsizing tents, scattering the grit from the gravel-banks with blinding force in every body's eyes, and sweeping furiously around every crook and corner in search of some sinner to smite. Never was such a wind as this—so scathing, so searching, so given to penetrate the very core of suffering humanity; disdaining overcoats, and utterly scornful of shawls and blankets. It actually seemed to double up, twist, pull, push, and screw the unfortunate biped till his muscles cracked and his bones rattled—following him wherever he sought refuge, pursuing him down the back of the neck, up the coat-sleeves, through the legs of his pantaloons, into his boots—in short, it was the most villainous and persecuting wind that ever blew. and I boldly protest that it did nobody good.

Yet, in the midst of the general wreck and crash of matter, the business of trading in claims, "bucking," and "bearing" went on as if the zephyrs of Virginia were as soft and balmy as those of San Francisco.

This was surely—no matter; nothing on earth could aspire to competition with such a place. It was essentially infernal in every aspect, whether viewed from the Comstock Ledge or the summit of Gold Hill. Nobody seemed to own the lots except by right of possession; yet there was trading in lots to an unlimited extent. Nobody had any money, yet every body was a millionaire in silver claims. Nobody had any credit, yet every body bought thousands of feet of glittering ore. Sales were made in the Mammoth, the Lady Bryant, the Sacramento, the Winnebunk, and the innumerable other "outside claims," at the most astounding figures but not a dime passed hands. All was silver underground, and deeds and mortgages on top; silver, silver everywhere, but scarce a dollar in coin. The small change had somehow gotten out of the hands of the public into the gambling saloons.

Every speck of ground covered by canvas, boards, baked mud, brush, or other architectural material, was jammed to suffocation; there were sleeping houses, twenty feet by thirty, in which from one hundred and fifty to two hundred solid sleepers sought slumber at night, at a dollar a head; tents, eight by ten, offering accommodations to the multitude; any thing or any place, even a stall in a stable, would have been a luxury.

The chief hotel, called, if I remember, the "Indication," or the "Hotel de Haystack," or some such euphonious name, professed to accommodate three hundred live men, and it doubtless did so, for the floors were covered from the attic to the solid earth—three hundred human beings in a tinder-box not bigger than a first-class hencoop! But they were sorry-looking sleepers as they came forth every morning, swearing at the evil genius who had directed them to this miserable spot—every man a dollar and a pound of flesh poorer. I saw some, who perhaps were short of means, take surreptious naps against the posts and walls in the bar-room, while they ostensibly professed to be mere spectators.

In truth, wherever I turned there was much to confirm the forebodings with which I had entered the Devil's Gate. The deep pits on the hill-sides; the blasted and barren appearance of the whole country; the unsightly hodge-podge of a town; the horrible confusion of tongues; the roaring, raving drunkards at the bar-rooms, swilling fiery liquids from morning till night; the flaring and flaunting gambling-saloons, filled with desperadoes of the vilest sort; the ceaseless torrent of imprecations that shocked the ear on every side; the mad speculations and feverish thirst for gain—all combined to give me a forcible impression of the unhallowed character of the place.

What dreadful savage is that? I asked, as a ferocious-looking monster in human shape stalked through the crowd. Is it—can it be the—No; that's only a murderer. He shot three men a few weeks ago, and will probably shoot another before night. And this aged and decrepit man, his thin locks floating around his haggard and un-shaved face, and matted with filth? That's a speculator from San Francisco. See how wildly he grasps at every "indication," as if he had a lease of life for a thousand years! And this bull-dog fellow, with a mutilated face, button-holing every by-passer? That fellow? Oh, he's only a "bummer" in search of a cocktail. And this—and this— all these crazy-looking wretches, running hither and thither with hammers and stones in their hands, calling one another aside, hurrying to the assay-offices, pulling out papers, exchanging mysterious signals—who and what are all these? Oh, these are Washoe millionaires. They are deep in "outside claims." The little fragments of rock they carry in their hands are "croppings" and "indications" from the "Wake-up-Jake," "Root-Hog-or-Die," "Wild Cat," "Grizzly Hill," "Dry-up," "Same Horse," "Let-her-Rip," "You Bet," "Gouge Eye," and other famous ledges and companies, in which they own some thousands of feet. Hold, good friend! I am convinced there is no rest for the wicked. All night long these dreadful noises continue; the ears are distracted with an unintelligible jargon of "croppings," "ledges," "lodes," "leads," "indications," "feet," and "strikes," and the nostrils offended with foul odors of boots, old pipes, and dirty blankets—who can doubt the locality? If the climate is more rigorous than Dante describes it, if Calypso might search in vain for Ulysses in such a motley crowd—these apparent differences are not inconsistent with the general theory of changes produced by American emigration and sudden conglomeration of such incongruous elements.

— Document No. 18 —

WESTERN TRANSPORTATION: THE BUTTERFIELD OVERLAND MAIL [18]

The swift spread of the mining frontier provided the United States government with a troublesome problem: how could the scattered camps be kept in touch with the East and with each other? Both western miners and eastern officials realized that this was necessary, the former because they were hungry for news of home and friends, the latter because they feared the growth of separatist sentiment if the West remained isolated. Congress found the answer in 1857 when it provided a large annual cash subsidy for any company that would run regular stage-coaches between California and the Mississippi Valley. The contract for this service was awarded by the Post-master General to a group of seasoned coachers organized as the Butterfield Overland Mail Company. By September, 1858, the company had built way-stations along the 2,812 mile route between Tipton, Missouri, the western terminus of the railroad, and San Francisco, each equipped with relays of horses or mules to pull the fast-moving coaches and "celerity wagons." The one passenger on the first westward trip of the Butterfield coaches was Waterman L. Ormsby, a correspondent of the New York Herald, *whose dispatches told the exciting story of the gruelling twenty-five day ordeal and triumphant arrival.*

[18] Ormsby's dispatches were first printed in the *New York Herald* between September 26 and November 19, 1858. They have also been collected in book form as Waterman L. Ormsby, *The Butterfield Overland Mail* (San Marino, California, 1942). The extract will be found on pp. 123-126.

As we entered the Pacheco Pass I had made up my mind to lie down in the wagon and take a nap, as night was fast approaching and I felt much fatigued. I heard the driver and agent, known throughout this section of the country as Tote Kinyon—the brother of the superintendent—remarking on the rough mountain pass which lay on our way; but, after the Guadalupe Pass, the Boston Mountain of the Ozark range, the Pacheco, and the New Pass, I had about concluded that I had seen all the mountain passes worth seeing on the route and that none could be more difficult or dangerous. But I was destined to be disappointed and to witness one of the finest views which the entire route affords.

The distance through the pass is twelve miles, and, instead of the cañon which I expected, I found the road to lead over hills piled on hills, which, though a little lower than their neighbors, were still at quite sufficient altitude. On every side we could look off down steep and craggy ravines, some of whose bottoms could not be discerned in the distance. Our road led immediately on the brink of many a precipice, over which a balky horse or a broken axle or an inexperienced driver might send us whirling in the air in a moment. There are also many abrupt curves in the road, winding around the sides of steep hills, on the edges of the ravines; many steep roads directly up and down the hills; and many rocks near the road, leaving just sufficient room for an experienced driver to take his team through without striking.

Most drivers would have been content to drive slowly over this spot—a distance of twelve miles and every foot of it requiring the most skillful management of the team to prevent the certain destruction of all in the coach. But our Jehu was in a hurry with the "first States' mail" and he was bound to put us through in good time. I suggested to him that a bad man riding on this road was on the very brink of the bad place and likely to depart thence at almost any moment if anything should break. He said, "Yes, but they didn't expect anything to break," and whipped up his horses just as we started down a steep hill. I expected to see him put down the brakes with all his might but he merely rested his foot on them, saying, "It's best to keep the wheels rolling, or they'll slide"; so he did keep the wheels rolling, and the whole coach slid down the steepest hills at the rate of fifteen—yes, twenty —miles an hour, now turning an abrupt curve with a whip and crack and "round the corner, Sally," scattering the loose stones, just grazing the rocks, sending its rattling echoes far away among the hills and ravines, frightening the slow teamsters on the road and making them haul off out of the way, and nearly taking away the breath of all.

The driver seemed to enjoy the fun, and invited me up to ride with him on the box. I got up, taking off my hat and throwing a blanket over my head; I held on tight as we dashed along—up and down, around the curves, and in straight lines, all at the same railroad speed. The loosening of a nut, the breaking of a strap, the shying of one of the four spirited horses, might—indeed would— have sent us all to "kingdom come," without a chance for saying prayers. But just as I made such a reflection, crack went the whip and away we flew, at a rate which I know would have made old John Butterfield, the president of the mail company, and a very experienced stage man, wish himself safely at home. For my part, I held on to the seat and held my breath, hoping we might get through safe. If I thought I was destined to be killed in a stage-coach I most certainly should have considered my time come.

We ran the twelve miles in an hour and five minutes, and, considering the ups and down, I thought it pretty good travelling. The mountain is covered with stunted oak trees, making it much resemble an orchard. On the east side I noticed very few rocks, and none large. On the west this was made up by huge rusty looking crags, towering high in air, or with heavy boulders on their sides or at their feet, as if just fallen. The road over the mountain is excellent for the place and is much improved by Mr. Firebaugh, who appears to be the enterprising man of the region. He has a toll gate at the base of the mountain, charging two dollars for the passage of a single four horse team, which is cheerfully paid in consideration of what he does to the road.

The next twenty miles, to Gilroy, we travelled in two hours, and took supper. The scene here was much like that at the other stopping places of any note along the route since we left Franklin. The villagers gathered around, asking all sorts of questions: "Have you got the States mail?" "What's the news from the States?" "Is the cable working yet?" "Have you got any through passengers?" "Only the correspondent of the *Herald*." "Why, then, we shall hear all about it." "How did you like your trip, sir?" "Very well." "How did you manage to sleep?" "What, slept in the wagons?" "Did you ride day and night?" "Well, I declare, I should think you would be tired." "Have plenty to eat?" "What, beans and jerked beef?" "Glad to hear you say they'd have better soon." "Meet any Injuns?" "None at all, eh?" "Well, that's some comfort." "How long have you been?" "Left St. Louis on the 16th of September." "Well, that beats all stage ridin." "Going to come through twice a week, eh?" "Well, that is good, now, ain't it?" "How's the line on the other end?" "Slow, eh?" "Of course, all the States people are slow." "Let 'em come out here and see a little life." "Here we do live—live fast, too."

— Document No. 19 —

THE FIRST TRANSCONTINENTAL RAILROAD: DRIVING THE FINAL SPIKE[19]

Stagecoaching was doomed almost from its beginning in the Far West, for by the 1850's railroading had developed to the point that a transcontinental line was

[19] J. D. B. Stillman, "The Last Tie," *Overland Monthly*, III (July, 1869), pp. 82-83.

*feasible. Inability of the North and South to agree upon
a route delayed construction until the South left the
Union with the start of the Civil War. Then two companies were chartered by Congress, the Union Pacific
to build westward from Omaha and the Central Pacific
to lay its tracks eastward from San Francisco. Work
progressed rapidly, with each company racing ahead
rapidly to collect as large a share as possible of the
generous federal grants and loans given for each mile of
construction. In May, 1869, their tracks met at Promontory, Utah, where the spanning of the continent was celebrated by driving in the last golden spike in an elaborate
ceremony. This was described by an eye-witness, J. D. B.
Stillman.*

✓   ✓   ✓

The munificence of private citizens of San Francisco
had contributed two gold spikes, each designed to be the
last one driven. Gentlemen from Nevada had contributed
a silver one, at whose forging a hundred men had each
struck a blow. The Governor of Arizona, also on behalf
of his Territory, had one of silver. The Laurel tie that
we brought with us was adjusted to its place; and in
order that each gold spike should be the *last,* one was
presented by Governor Stanford, President of the Central
Pacific, to Vice President Durant, of the Union Pacific,
who should drive it as the last on the latter road, while
the other was to be the last on the Central road, and be
driven last of all by Governor Stanford, who had thrown
the first shovelful of earth at the opening of the road.

It had been arranged with Mr. Gamble, superintendent
of the telegraph lines, that throughout the cities of the
United States, wherever fire-alarm telegraphs were established, connection should be made with the last spike
and the hammer that drove it, so that the blow should
announce itself and fire cannon on the shores of both
oceans at the same instant. Preparations having been completed, the operator sent notice to all stations throughout
the country to be ready, and the whole nation held its
breath. A reverend gentleman present was invited to
invoke the blessing of Almighty God upon the work.
The operator announced: "Hats off, prayer is being said";

and as we uncovered our heads, the crowds that were gathered at the various telegraph offices in the land uncovered theirs. The prayer ended, the silver spikes were driven. Durant drove his of gold. Stanford stood with the silver sledge gleaming in the air, whose blow was to be heard farther, without metaphor, than any blow struck by mortal man; the realization of the ancient myth of Jupiter with the thunderbolt in his hand. The blow fell, and simultaneously the roar of cannon on both shores of the continent announced the tidings: *It is done!* The alarm bells of the principal cities struck, one—two— three—synchronous with the strokes of the hammer; and people rushed from their houses, thinking a general alarm of fire was being rung. The cause soon became known, and banners everywhere were flung to the breeze; other bells joined in the cry of joy and of triumph. *Te Deum Laudamus* was sung in the churches, and the chimes rung out the national anthems. The nation made a day of it.

— Document No. 20 —

GREAT PLAINS INDIAN WARFARE: THE CHIVINGTON MASSACRE[20]

The advance of the mining frontier and the criss-crossing of the Great Plains by stagecoach and railroad lines plunged the United States into its last and most brutal Indian wars. As the red men were elbowed from their hunting grounds by miners or watched the slaughter of the buffalo herds by scores of hunters, they took to the warpath to preserve not only their lives but their way of life. One of the most tragic episodes in the decade of

[20] *U. S. Senate, Reports of Committees,* 39th Cong., 2nd Sess., Doc. No. 156, pp. 53, 73-74.

warfare that began in the 1860's was the Chivington Massacre. This occurred when the Cheyenne and Arapaho Indians resisted the federal government's orders to give up their tribal lands and retreat to the barren Sand Creek reservation in eastern Colorado. For a time their raiding parties devastated the Colorado frontier before they sued for peace and retreated to their reservation. There they were surprised on November 29, 1864, by an army of militiamen under Colonel J. M. Chivington. Even the seasoned soldiers were horrified by the slaughter of five hundred red men, women and children that followed, as two of them testified before a congressional investigating committee.

✓ ✓ ✓

Our battalion was attached to the command of Colonel J. M. Chivington, and left Fort Lyon on the night of the 28th of November, 1864; about daybreak on the morning of the 29th of November we came in sight of the camp of the friendly Indians aforementioned, and were ordered by Colonel Chivington to attack the same, which was accordingly done. The command of Colonel Chivington was composed of about one thousand men; the village of the Indians consisted of from one hundred to one hundred and thirty lodges, and, as far as I am able to judge, of from five hundred to six hundred souls, the majority of which were women and children; in going over the battle-ground the next day I did not see a body of man, woman, or child but was scalped, and in many instances their bodies were mutilated in the most horrible manner—men, women, and children's privates cut out, &c; I heard one man say that he had cut out a woman's private parts and had them for exhibition on a stick; I heard another man say that he had cut the fingers off an Indian to get the rings on the hand; according to the best of my knowledge and belief these atrocities that were committed were with knowledge of J. M. Chivington, and I do not know of his taking any measures to prevent them; I heard of one instance of a child a few months old being thrown in the feed-box of a wagon, and after being carried some distance left on the ground to perish; I also heard of numerous instances in which men had cut out the private parts of females and stretched them over the saddle-bows, and wore them over their hats while riding in the ranks. . . .

We arrived at the Indian village about daylight. On arriving in sight of the village a battalion of the 1st cavalry and the Fort Lyon battalion were ordered on a charge to surround the village and the Indian herd. After driving the herd towards the village, Lieutenant Wilson's battalion of the 1st took possession of the northeast side of the village, Major Anthony's battalion took position on the south, Colonel Chivington's 3d regiment took position in our rear, dismounted, and after the fight had been commenced by Major Anthony and Lieutenant Wilson, mounted, and commenced firing through us and over our heads. About this time, Captain John Smith, Indian interpreter, attempting to come to our troops, was fired on by our men, at the command of some one in our rear, "To shoot the damned old son of a bitch." One of my men rode forward to save him, but was killed. To get out of the fire from the rear, we were ordered to the left. About this time Colonel Chivington moved his regiment to the front, the Indians retreating up the creek, and hiding under the banks. There seemed to be no organization among our troops; every one on his own hook and shots flying between our own ranks. White Antelope ran towards our columns unarmed, and with both arms raised, but was killed. Several other of the warriors were killed in like manner. The women and children were huddled together, and most of our fire was concentrated on them. Sometimes during the engagement I was compelled to move my company to get out of the fire of our own men. Captain Soule did not order his men to fire when the order was given to commence the fight. During the fight, the battery on the opposite side of the creek kept firing at the bank while our men were in range. The Indian warriors, about one hundred in number, fought desperately; there were about five hundred all told. I estimated the loss of the Indians to be from one hundred and twenty-five to one hundred and seventy-five killed; no wounded fell into our hands and all the dead were scalped. The Indian who was pointed out as White Antelope had his fingers cut off. Our force was so large that there was no necessity of firing on the Indians. They did not return the fire until after our troops had fired several rounds. We had the assurance from Major Anthony that Black Kettle and his friends should be saved, and only those Indians who had committed depradations should be harmed. During the fight no officer took any measures to get out of the fire of our own men. Left Hand stood with his arms folded, saying he would not fight the white men, as they were his friends. I told Colonel Chivington of the position in which the officers stood from Major Wynkoop's pledges to the Indians, and also Major Anthony's, and that it would be murder, in every sense of the word, if he attacked those Indians. His reply was, bringing his fist down close to my face, "Damn any man who sympathizes with Indians." I told him what pledges were given the Indians. He replied, "That he had come to kill Indians, and believed it to be honorable to kill Indians under any and all circumstances"; all this at Fort Lyon. Lieutenant Dunn went to Colonel Chivington and wanted to know if he could kill his prisoner, young Smith. His reply was, "Don't ask me; you know my orders, I want no prisoners." Colonel Chivington was in a position where he must have seen the scalping and mutilation going on. One of the soldiers was taking a squaw prisoner across the creek, when other soldiers fired on him, telling him they would kill him if he did not let her go. On our approach to the village I saw some one with a white flag approaching our lines, and the troops fired upon it; and at the time Captain Smith was fired upon, some one wearing a uniform coat was fired upon approaching our lines. Captain Smith was wearing one. After the fight I saw the United States flag in the Indian camp. It is a mistake that there were any white scalps found in the village. I saw one, but it was very old, the hair being much faded. I was ordered to burn the village, and was through all the lodges. There was not any snow on the ground, and no rifle-pits. . . .

— Document No. 21 —

SPREAD OF THE CATTLE FRONTIER: THE ROUND UP[21]

The outcome of the Indian wars was inevitable. One by one the beaten tribes were herded onto reservations and their lands thrown open to settlers. First to capitalize on this opportunity were the cattlemen, who recognized in the government-owned lands of the Great Plains a giant pasture where longhorns driven northward from Texas could multiply with little cost. Between 1870 and 1887 that whole vast land, larger than half of Europe, was appropriated by ranchers, while the cowboy was plummeted into fame as the hero of dime novels and "westerns." Like all frontiersmen, the cattlemen devised unique institutions to care for their distinctive problems. Of these none was more colorful than the "round up," described by an English traveler who lived for a time as a cowboy.

✓   ✓   ✓

At last we are ready; our boss gives final instructions with regard to the circle each man will have to ride, and the exact spot towards which we are to converge by midday. No, we are not off yet; look at yon dun broncho ridden by a young hand; his stride is short and jerky, he is fetching at his bridle in an ominous manner, his ears laid back, and his long tail tight between his hind quarters; should he succeed in getting his head down or detect the slightest symptom of nervousness in his rider, we shall see some fun. He stops, shies half round, and with a vicious squeal pitches high into the air; his rider is already clutching the horn of his saddle, another buck and he is

---

[21] John Baumann "On a Western Ranche," *The Fortnightly Review*, N.S. XLI (March, 1887), 523-525.

hanging on by the mane, yet another, and he is sprawling on the ground. Yoicks, gone away! We all gallop after the riderless brute, swinging our lassoes exultingly round our heads, and in a few minutes he is dragged sullenly back to his crestfallen rider, who with his blood now fairly roused, remounts full of vengeful resolve, and this time succeeds in proving himself master.

But now to our work. We cross the river at a wild spot where its banks are formed by steep bluffs studded with cactus and prickly pear; cypress, cedar, and maple nestling at their base. A steep, narrow gorge leads to wide plains, bounded by a low range of flat-topped antelope hills. Up this gorge the circle-riders make their way, and dividing into couples, start at a lope for the lurking-places of the cattle. Creek, shady cañon, and arroyo are searched, and after many a chase after wilful calf or sullen bull, a goodly round up of seven or eight hundred head is formed.

"So—o, so—o, so gently, lads; hold them together! Gallop round them; head back that little column led by a frightened steer. Quick! quick! or by the powers the whole herd will be off." Good! our little cow-ponies can go like the wind for a short distance; can turn and twist, and stop in the twinkling of an eye (sharper, indeed, than suits the seat of an awkward horseman); the fugitives are pressed back, bellowing loud protest the while. But now the whole mass is violently agitated; a couple of sharp-horned Texan bulls have come foul of each other. Quickly a space is cleared around them; they stand face to face glaring and snorting, with heads lowered, and defiantly tearing up clouds of dust till one or the other rushes to the attack. With a crash their heads meet; they sway about for a moment with locked horns; separate, retreat, and dash together again forehead to forehead, with all their strength and fury concentrated into that ferocious collision, until at length, after a combat lasting several minutes, the weaker turns tail and leaves his victor triumphant.

It is a wild and variegated spectacle, this mass of tangled and tossing horns. Rough, poor-looking cows, with calves as pretty as paint; savage, long-horned Texans; handsome, bald-faced Herefords; big, black, hornless

Galloways; broad-browed shorthorn bulls, all thorough-breds, intermingle with nondescript grades of all sizes and ages. They have not yet quite shed their winter coats, or the big brands on shoulder, side, and hip would stand out more distinctly. They are ear-marked in every conceivable manner, from the becoming underslope to the disfiguring grub, which leaves a mere stump in the place of an ear. All are in lean condition, not having filled out yet on the juicy and fattening grasses which will shortly ripen as the season advances, but they look bright-eyed, clean, and healthy, with the exception of a few locoed beasts, whose dull, stupid eyes, mangy coats, and clumsy, purposeless movements, prove them to have indulged in orgies of the fatal plant. . . .

Tom Connor, range foreman of some fifty thousand head of cattle, is for the moment our "big chief," for it is on his ground that we are working. Tall, good-looking, and somewhat of a prairie "dude" in appearance, he is now the centre of a group of men awaiting his instructions. Some half-a-dozen of these, mounted on well-trained cutting-ponies, proceed quietly to enter the herd and wind their way in and out among the cattle until they mark one of their own brands. With a smart cut from the raw-hide quirt a young steer is set in motion; whichever way he twists or turns he find the relentless horseman at his heels, and is forced against his will to the outskirts of the herd. Why should he leave his companions? He makes a sudden desperate turn, and rushes among them again. Before the eager little pony has had time to follow, he has succeeded in diving well into their midst. Leave him there for the present; he is on the alert now, and will be "mean to cut"; these youngsters, be they bull, heifer, or steer, always are. Others have been more successful; animals are being separated from the main bunch on all sides, and sent trotting in the direction of the respective cuts.

It is an animated, blood-stirring scene. The cuts are "held" by cowboys, who are tearing about in their endeavours to keep the beasts together. The cutting-ponies are dodging and turning with marvellous rapidity and sagacity, appearing almost to anticipate the movements of the pursued. The air is filled with smoke-like clouds of dust and the ground trembles with the thunder of many hoofs. By the time the sun nears the horizon the big round-up has been divided into several bunches, which are being slowly moved to their respective bedding-grounds, there to be held by night guards until the following day, when they will be day-herded and driven to our next camping-place. Both men and horses are dog-tired. We have changed our mounts after the mid-day meal, it is true, but the ground is rough, the work has been fast and furious. Our wiry little ponies, standing barely over fourteen hands, have to carry saddles weighing full forty pounds, and in many cases big, strapping fellows who, riding purely by balance and with a loose seat, are all over their backs, when the clever little animals dart about after cattle. They are, besides, roughly used, getting no praise or encouragement for work willingly done, but whip, spurs, and oaths for the slightest mistake. One form of suffering so common to their kind they certainly do escape. Their riders are light of hand, the enormous Mexican spade-bit hangs loosely in their mouths, and it is but rarely that they are made to realise its full power. Their heads are now turned towards camp, and they make an effort to gallop in gaily. We off-saddle and coil up our lariats to catch our night-horses out of the bunch which the horse-rustler is holding in readiness for us, saddle them, stake them out, and leave them there until our turn comes to go out on "night guard"; hobble the remainder of the bunch and let them wander off at their own sweet will. The day's work is done!

— Document No. 22 —

THE FARMERS' LAST FRONTIER: WHEAT GROWING ON THE GREAT PLAINS[22]

The cattleman reigned as king of the West for only a short time; as railroads, improved farm machinery, and dry-farming techniques allowed the agricultural conquest of the Great Plains to begin, the ranchers were pushed slowly westward by the steady advance of small farmers. The problems that faced them as they transformed that gargantuan grassland into fertile fields of yellow grain were many. These were described by a traveler in the plains area of Minnesota who could as well have been picturing scenes in the Dakotas, Nebraska, or Kansas.

✦   ✦   ✦

As one goes over the country in the fall of the year he sees vast tracts of "new breaking," where the virgin soil, black as ink, and rich almost to glutinousness, has been broken by the plow, and the soil turned bottom upward in long, dark bands or layers as far as the eye can reach. Here it is exposed for months to the wind and weather till it decomposes and becomes fit for agricultural purposes. Every year vast tracts of prairie are thus turned over, or "broken," and with the next the loam is leveled and the seed is cast in; and thus large additions are annually made to the aggregate amount of acres of wheat.

Take your stand on one of these "new breaking-pieces," and look perhaps in any direction, and you will find yourself enclosed by its dreary strips of black loam; not a blade of grass nor a single leaf will appear. It is a picture of

[22] "Among the Wheat-Fields of Minnesota," *Harper's New Monthly Magazine*, CCXII (January, 1868), pp. 193-194.

desolation and vacancy; nature and life are in their embryo; not a glimpse can be seen of their future creations. Nothing can exceed the contrast between this and what these same fields will present a year or two afterward, when they stand yellow with the harvest, an emblem of cheerfulness and prosperity.

Farms are generally 160 acres in extent—a "quarter section" being usually the quantity bought and worked. Under the Homestead Law lands are constantly taken up, the cost being a mere trifle for fees, etc. The settler is required to locate on it, put up a small house, do some fencing and "breaking," and pass a night on it at least once every six months.

Many amusing stories are told how persons of ingenious habits of mind and India-rubber consciences manage to conform to the letter, while they evade the more burdensome intents of the law. The merest apology for a house, and the least possible amount of residence and "improvements" are done. Still this dodging of the law works no serious violation of its contemplated objects. Lands are opened, destitute families are provided with a farm and means of attaining independence and prosperity, and the State is settled up. Sometimes a family is so constituted as to be able to take four quarters, or a full square mile of land. No single applicant can take out papers for more than one quarter section, and a man and his wife and young children are viewed as one party. But if he has a widowed mother and two unmarried sisters grown up living with him, each is regarded as a legal applicant; and they arrange it often thus: They select four quarter sections lying contiguous to each other, and put up a house right upon the centre where the four quarter sections touch, so that each quarter of the building stands on a different quarter section. Partitions divide the interior into rooms to correspond; and each party then fulfills his obligations to the law at one-fourth the expense he or she would otherwise incur. They are supposed to form four distinct families, dwelling apart, although practically they still form but one household as before.

These wild lands thus entered are worth about $5 per acre, and when "improved" rise to $15 or $25 according to circumstances. At the end of five years' residence Gov-

ernment gives a clean deed of the property. Many, however, having the means, prefer to buy the land outright at
the start, paying the Government price, $1.25 per acre.

Wheat matures from about the beginning to the middle
of August. The whole country then awakens from its long
slothfulness. Business revives. Interest, energy, and happiness every where appear. No one who has never witnessed
the dullness pervading all departments of business during
the winter and spring can comprehend the great and
sudden transformation which the incoming crop produces.
Mechanics, tradesmen, wheat-buyers, railroads, steamboats—all seem to be indued with new life and vigor:
every where is activity, bustle, and confusion. . . .

— Document No. 23 —

THE CLOSING OF THE FRONTIER:
THE BOOMER RUSH
TO OKLAHOMA[23]

*As the Great Plains filled with farmers during the
1870's and 1880's, land-hungry westerners were soon
casting covetous eyes on the Indian reservations. Their
first objective was the "Oklahoma District," an unoccupied
island of some two million acres lying near the middle of
what is today Oklahoma. Although this was surrounded
by the lands of the twenty-two tribes that had been
crowded into the Indian Territory, western "Boomers"
demanded that it be thrown open to settlement. Their
pressure grew so insistent during the 1880's that Congress
finally backed down; early in 1889 the President an-*

[23] *The Nation,* XLVIII (April 4, 1889), p. 280.

nounced that at noon on April 22, the Oklahoma District would be opened to homesteaders. For weeks before that day every trail leading toward Oklahoma was crowded with eager homeseekers. The scene was described by the correspondent of an eastern journal.

✓   ✓   ✓

There is probably nowhere else in the world such a curious collection of settlements as are now stretched along the border lines of the new Territory waiting for the 22d of April to arrive. They have regular names, like Beaver City and Purcell, with hotels and stores. Some of them have a population of 1,500, and at one store the gross receipts in a single day are said to have reached $500. Yet there is scarcely a permanent building in any of them. One town is famous for having a plastered house in which the railway agent lives. For the most part the boomers are living in dug-outs, or sod houses, with some rough wooden shanties and many tents. Yet business is carried on regularly, and there is a scale of rentals ranging from $5 to $25 a year. Clothing is the most difficult thing to obtain, and the 10,000 boomers who are thus waiting on the threshold of the promised land are clad more like Indians than civilized people. In addition to these 10,000, there are said to be many thousands more in the regular towns and settlements near the border, and it is estimated that the new Territory may have a population of 100,000 a few months after it is thrown open for settlement. . . .

— Document No. 24 —

OPENING THE OKLAHOMA DISTRICT: THE GREATEST FOOT RACE IN HISTORY[24]

When the troops who had been stationed in the Oklahoma District to hold back illegal early entries, or "Sooners," finally fired their guns in air just at noon on April 22, 1889, the greatest race for land in all American history began. The nearly 100,000 persons who had lined the borders surged forward, some on horseback, some in wagons, some on foot, some in the fifteen railroad trains that had been lined up on the tracks of the Santa Fé Railroad which crossed the district. Within a few hours of turmoil, confusion, and heartbreak, the whole region was occupied; the thousands who lost out in the race could console themselves that their pressure would soon force the government to open the rest of the Indian Territory reservations to homesteaders. In this frantic, unreasoning quest for farms lay proof that westerners knew that the end of the frontier was at hand, and that the era of cheap government lands was drawing to a close. A participant reflected this attitude as he described the Oklahoma rush.

As our train slowly moved through the Cherokee strip, a vast procession of "boomers" was seen moving across the plains to the Oklahoma lines, forming picturesque groups on the otherwise unbroken landscape. The wagon road through the "strip," extemporized by the boomers, ran for long distances parallel with the railway, and the procession that extended the whole distance illustrated

[24] Hamilton S. Wicks, "The Opening of Oklahoma," *The Cosmopolitan,* VII (September, 1889), 464-468.

the characteristic of western American life. Here, for instance, would be a party consisting of a "prairie schooner" drawn by four scrawny, raw-boned horses, and filled with a tatterdemalion group, consisting of a shaggy-bearded man, a slatternly-looking woman, and several girls and boys, faithful images of their parents, in shabby attire, usually with a dog and a coop of chickens. In striking contrast to this frontier picture, perhaps a couple of flashy real-estate men from Wichita would come jogging on a short distance behind, driving a spanking span of bays, with an equipage looking for all the world as though it had just come from a fashionable livery stable. Our train, whirling rapidly over the prairie, overtook many such contrasted pictures. There were single rigs and double rigs innumerable; there were six-mule teams and four-in-hands, with here and there parties on horseback, and not a few on foot, trudging along the wayside. The whole procession marched, rode, or drove, as on some gala occasion, with smiling faces and waving hands. Every one imagined that Eldorado was just ahead, and I dare say the possibility of failure or disappointment did not enter into the consideration of a single individual on that cool and delightful April day. For many, alas, the anticipations were "April hopes, the fools of chance."

As our train neared the Oklahoma border the "procession" became more dense, and in some instances clogged the approaches to the fords of the small streams that crossed its pathway. When we finally slowed up at the dividing line the camps of the "boomers" could be seen extending in every direction, and a vast amount of stock was strewn over the green prairie.

And now the hour of twelve was at hand, and every one on the *qui vive* for the bugle blast that would dissolve the chain of enchantment hitherto girding about this coveted land. Many of the "boomers" were mounted on high-spirited and fleet-footed horses, and had ranged themselves along the territorial line, scarcely restrained even by the presence of the troop of cavalry from taking summary possession. The better class of wagons and carriages ranged themselves in line with the horsemen, and even here and there mule teams attached to canvas-covered vehicles stood in the front ranks, with the reins and whip grasped by the "boomers' " wives. All was excitement and expectation. Every nerve was on tension and every muscle strained. The great event for which these brawny noblemen of the West have been waiting for years was on the point of transpiring. Suddenly the air was pierced with the blast of a bugle. Hundreds of throats echoed the sound with shouts of exultation. The quivering limbs of saddled steeds, no longer restrained by the hands that held their bridles, bounded forward simultaneously into the "beautiful land" of Oklahoma; and wagons and carriages and buggies and prairie schooners and a whole congregation of curious equipages joined in this unparalleled race, where every starter was bound to win a prize—the "Realization Stakes" of home and prosperity.

Here was a unique contest in which thousands participated and which was to occur but once for all time. Truly an historical event! We, the spectators, witnessed the spectacle with most intense interest. Away dashed the thoroughbreds, the bronchos, the pintos, and the mustangs at a breakneck pace across the uneven surface of the prairie. It was amazing to witness the recklessness of those cow-boy riders: they jumped obstacles; they leaped ditches; they cantered with no diminution of speed through water-pools; and when they came to a ravine too wide to leap, down they would go with a rush, and up the other side with a spurt of energy, to scurry once more like mad over the level plain. This reckless riding was all very well at the fore part of the race, but it could not prevail against the more discreet maneuverings of several elderly "boomers" who rode more powerful and speedy horses. One old white-bearded fellow especially commanded attention. He was mounted on a coal-black thoroughbred, and avoided any disaster by checking the pace of his animal when ravines had to be crossed. But his splendid bursts of speed when no obstructions barred the way soon placed him far in advance of all his competitors. It took but a short time to solve this question of speed among the riders, and after a neck-and-neck race for half a mile or more they spread like a fan over the prairie, and were eventually lost to our vision among the rolling billows of Oklahoma's far-expanding prairie.

The occupants of our train now became absorbed in

their own fate. Indeed our train was one of the participants in this unexampled race, and, while watching the
scurrying horsemen, we ourselves had been gliding
through the picturesque landscape. It was rather hard
pulling for our engine until we reached the apex of the
heavy grade that commanded a view of the Cimarron
Valley, spread out in picturesque beauty at our very feet.
Our train now rushed along down grade with the speed
of a limited express—crossing the fine bridge that spans the
Cimarron with a roar, and swinging around the hills that
intervened between the river and the Guthrie town site
with the rapidity of a swallow's flight. All that there was
of Guthrie, the now famous "magic city" on April 22d, at
1:30 P.M., when the first train from the north drew up at
the station and unloaded its first instalment of settlers,
was a water-tank, a small station-house, a shanty for the
Wells, Fargo Express, and a Government Land Office—
a building twenty by forty feet, hastily constructed five
hundred feet from the depot, on the brow of the gently-
sloping acclivity that stretches eastward from the railway
track. It is true that a handful of enterprising United States
deputy marshals, a few railroad boys, and one or two
newspaper correspondents had already surveyed and
staked out several hundred acres of town site, and had,
by way of maintaining their claims to this extensive property, erected a few tents here and there in the neighborhood of the Land Office building. The imbecile policy
of the government in the manner of opening the new
Territory for settlement invited just this sort of enterprise.
But when the hundreds of people from our train and the
thousands from following trains arrived, they "coppered
the situation," to speak in Western parlance, with very
little consideration for the privileges, interests, or rights
of the deputies and their friends.

I remember throwing my blankets out of the car window the instant the train stopped at the station. I remember tumbling after them through the self-same window.
Then I joined the wild scramble for a town lot up the
sloping hillside at a pace discounting any "go-as-you-
please" race. There were several thousand people con-
verging on the same plot of ground, each eager for a
town lot which was to be acquired without cost or without

price, each solely dependent on his own efforts, and
animated by a spirit of fair play and good humor.

The race was not over when you reached the particular
lot you were content to select for your possession. The
contest was still who should drive their stakes first, who
would erect their little tents soonest, and then, who would
quickest build a little wooden shanty.

The situation was so peculiar that it is difficult to con-
vey correct impressions of the situation. It reminded me
of playing blindman's-bluff. One did not know how far
to go before stopping; it was hard to tell when it was best
to stop, and it was a puzzle whether to turn to the right
or the left. Every one appeared dazed, and all for the most
acted like a flock of stray sheep. Where the boldest led,
many others followed. I found myself, without exactly
knowing how, about midway between the government
building and depot. It occurred to me that a street would
probably run past the depot. I accosted a man who looked
like a deputy, and asked him if this was to be a street
along here.

"Yes," he replied. "We are laying off four corner lots
right here for a lumber yard."

"Is this the corner where I stand?" I inquired.

"Yes," he responded, approaching me.

"Then I claim this corner lot!" I said with decision, as
I jammed my location stick in the ground and hammered
it securely home with my heel. "I propose to have one lot
at all hazards on this town site, and you will have to limit
yourself to three, in this location at least."

An angry altercation ensued, but I stoutly maintained
my position, and my rights. I proceeded at once to unstrap
a small folding cot I brought with me, and by standing it
on its end it made a tolerable center-pole for a tent. I
then threw a couple of my blankets over the cot, and
staked them securely into the ground on either side. Thus
I had a claim that was unjumpable because of substantial
improvements, and I felt safe and breathed more freely
until my brother arrived on the third train, with our tent
and equipments. Not long after his arrival, an enterprising
individual came driving by with a plow, and we hired him
for a dollar to plow around the lot I had stepped off,
twenty-five feet in front and one hundred and forty feet

in depth. Before dusk we had a large wall tent erected on our newly-acquired premises, with a couple of cots inside and a liberal amount of blankets for bedding. Now we felt doubly secure in our possession, and as night approached I strolled up on the eminence near the land office, and surveyed the wonderful cyclorama spread out before me on all sides. Ten thousand people had "squatted" upon a square mile of virgin prairie that first afternoon, and as the myriad of white tents suddenly appeared upon the face of the country, it was as though a vast flock of huge white-winged birds had just settled down upon the hillsides and in the valleys. Here indeed was *a city laid out and populated in half a day*. Thousands of camp-fires sparkled upon the dark bosom of the prairie as far as the eye could reach, and there arose from this huge camp a subdued hum declaring that this almost innumerable multitude of the brave and self-reliant men had come to stay and work, and build in that distant Western wilderness a city that should forever be a trophy to American enterprise and daring.

A FEW BOOKS ABOUT THE WEST

Any serious study of the history of America's frontier should begin with a reading of the germinal essays by Frederick Jackson Turner, written at the turn of the century and collected in his *The Frontier in American History* (New York, 1920). The two most widely used general books describing the westward movement are Robert E. Riegel, *America Moves West* (New York, 1930, rev., 1955), and Ray A. Billington, *Westward Expansion* (New York, 1949, rev., 1959).

Scholarly studies of the southern colonial frontier are few, but Thomas P. Abernethy, *Three Virginia Frontiers* (University, La., 1941), and Verner W. Crane, *The Southern Frontier* (Durham, 1928), are notable exceptions. The unique New England land system is explained in Roy H. Akagi, *The Town Proprietors of the New England Colonies* (Philadelphia, 1924), and William Haller, *The Puritan Frontier* (New York, 1951), while Lois K. Mathews, *The Expansion of New England* (Boston, 1909), treats that subject briefly. Pontiac's Rebellion is well described in Howard H. Peckham, *Pontiac and the Indian Uprising* (Princeton, 1947). The movement of settlers into western Pennsylvania before the Revolution is traced in Solon J. and Elizabeth H. Buck, *The Planting of Civilization in Western Pennsylvania* (Pittsburgh, 1939), into eastern Tennessee in Thomas P. Abernethy, *From Frontier to Plantation in Tennessee* (Chapel Hill, 1932), and into Kentucky in John Bakeless, *Daniel Boone* (New York, 1939), and Kathryn H. Mason, *James Harrod of Kentucky* (Baton Rouge, 1950).

A scholarly work on the West's role in causing the Revolution is Thomas P. Abernethy, *Western Lands and the American Revolution* (New York, 1937), while warfare along the frontiers is described in James A. James, *George Rogers Clark* (Chicago, 1928), and Francis W. Halsey, *The Old New York Frontier* (New York, 1901). Paul C. Phillips, *The West in the Diplomacy of the Ameri-*

can Revolution (Urbana, 1913), is particularly important for its account of the peace negotiations. Roy M. Robbins, *Our Landed Heritage* (Princeton, 1942), deals with the origins and development of the national land system and Randolph C. Downes, *Council Fires on the Upper Ohio* (Pittsburgh, 1940), with Indian warfare in the Ohio Valley. Diplomatic conflicts in the Old Southwest are described in Arthur P. Whitaker, *The Spanish-American Frontier, 1783-1795* (Boston, 1927), and *The Mississippi Question, 1795-1803* (New York, 1934). The occupation of the trans-Appalachian country is the theme of Paul D. Evans, *The Holland Land Company* (Buffalo, 1924), Beverley W. Bond, Jr., *The Civilization of the Old Northwest* (New York, 1934), and John W. Barnhard, *Valley of Democracy* (Bloomington, Ind., 1953). Julius W. Pratt, *Expansionists of 1812* (New York, 1925), and Glenn Tucker, *Tecumseh: Vision of Glory* (Indianapolis, 1956), help explain why frontiersmen goaded the United States into the War of 1812.

The peopling of the Old Northwest in the years after 1815 is described in R. C. Buley, *The Old Northwest, Pioneer Period, 1815-1840* (2 vols., Indianapolis, 1950) and more briefly in chapters in Frederick Jackson Turner, *Rise of the New West, 1819-1828* (New York, 1906), and *The United States, 1830-1850* (New York, 1935). No comparable studies dealing with the Old Southwest exist, although Everett Dick, *The Dixie Frontier* (New York, 1948), contains information on social conditions.

General works dealing with the early occupation of the Trans-Mississippi West include Cardinal Goodwin, *The Trans-Mississippi West* (New York, 1922), W. J. Ghent, *The Early Far West* (New York, 1931), and Ray A. Billington, *The Far Western Frontier, 1830-1860* (New York, 1956). The Santa Fé trade is adequately studied in R. L. Duffus, *The Santa Fé Trail* (New York, 1930). On the fur trade Hiram M. Chittenden, *The American Fur Trade of the Far West* (3 vols., New York, 1902, rev., 1935), is a pioneering work while Bernard DeVoto, *Across the Wide Missouri* (Boston, 1947), is popular. More scholarly are two later books: Dale L. Morgan, *Jedediah Smith and the Opening of the West* (Indianapolis, 1953), and

Robert G. Cleland, *This Reckless Breed of Men* (New York, 1950), which deals with the Southwest.

American migration into Texas is described in Eugene C. Barker, *The Life of Stephen F. Austin* (Nashville, 1925), while William C. Binkley, *The Texas Revolution* (Baton Rouge, 1952), is an interpretative study of that event and William R. Hogan, *The Texas Republic* (Norman, 1946), an account of the life during independence. Overland migration is sketched in Jay Monaghan, *The Overland Trail* (Indianapolis, 1937), although its sections on Oregon migration should be supplemented with W. J. Ghent, *The Road to Oregon* (New York, 1929). George R. Stewart, *Ordeal by Hunger* (New York, 1936), graphically describes the tribulations of the Donner party. The diplomatic results of expansion are the themes of Joseph W. Schmitz, *Texan Statecraft, 1836-1845* (San Antonio, 1945), and Melvin C. Jacobs, *Winning Oregon* (Caldwell, Idaho, 1938).

Migration into Utah after the Mexican War is described in Nels Anderson, *Desert Saints: The Mormon Frontier in Utah* (Chicago, 1942), and Milton R. Hunter, *Brigham Young the Colonizer* (Salt Lake City, 1940). Two scholarly accounts of the gold rush of 1849 and of mining in California are John W. Caughey, *Gold Is the Cornerstone* (Berkeley, 1948), and Rodman W. Paul, *California Gold* (Cambridge, 1947). The northward advance of the mining frontier is treated in William J. Trimble, *The Mining Advance Into the Inland Empire* (Madison, 1914), while Grant H. Smith, *The History of the Comstock Lode* (Reno, 1943), is the only adequate study of that area.

Western freighting is vividly depicted in Raymond W. and Mary L. Settle, *Empire on Wheels* (Stanford, 1939), and western stagecoaching in Oscar O. Winther, *Via Western Express & Stagecoach* (Stanford, 1950). J. V. Frederick, *Ben Holladay* deals with the last days of coaching; the early railroads that doomed the coaches are treated in Robert E. Riegel, *The Story of the Western Railroads* (New York, 1926).

The Indian wars that opened the Great Plains to settlement are colorfully pictured in Paul I. Wellman, *Death on the Prairie* (New York, 1934), and the extermination of the buffalo that meant defeat for the red men in Mari Sandoz, *The Buffalo Hunters* (New York, 1954). Loring B. Priest, *Uncle Sam's Stepchildren* (New Brunswick, 1942), traces the evolution of Indian policy. The spread of the cattle industry is described in Ernest S. Osgood, *The Day of the Cattlemen* (Minneapolis, 1929), and Edward E. Dale, *The Range Cattle Industry* (Norman, 1930). Ranching and farming in the Southwest are discussed in Rupert N. Richardson, *The Greater Southwest* (Glendale, Calif., 1935), and Carl C. Rister, *The Southwestern Frontier, 1865-1881* (Cleveland, 1928), and in the Northwest in Harold E. Briggs, *Frontiers of the Northwest* (New York, 1940). Essential to an understanding of the farmers' frontier on the plains is Walter P. Webb, *The Great Plains* (Boston, 1931); Fred A. Shannon, *The Farmers' Last Frontier* (New York, 1945), deals with the same subject in a more orthodox manner. Everett Dick, *The Sod-House Frontier* (New York, 1937), pictures the life of plains' farmers. The rush into the Oklahoma country is described in Carl C. Rister, *Land Hunger: David L. Payne and the Oklahoma Boomers* (Norman, 1942).

INDEX

VAN NOSTRAND ANVIL BOOKS already published